Do-Tell

To order additional copies, please contact us.
BookSurge, LLC
www.booksurge.com
1-866-308-6235
orders@booksurge.com

RAY L. RUBY

DO-TELL

HEAR THE CORN GROW

2005

Do-Tell

The words written below and on the following pages are dedicated to my beloved wife JANE, and to our children, RITA, JEAN, JOHN, ALAN, PAUL, GERY, MARY, LORI and all of our grandchildren. I love all of you very much.

DRIFT BACK INTO THE YEARS NOW PASSED
THE CORRIDORS OF LONG AGO
WALK WITH ME, AS I REMEMBER
THROUGH THESE PAGES, AS I SHOW

THE VALLEYS INTO WHICH I'VE WANDERED
THE PATHWAYS WHICH I CHOSE TO TROD
THE RULES WHICH I HAVE TRIED TO HONOR
OF MY COUNTRY AND OUR GOD

WHEN LIFE'S RIVER CEASES FLOWING
AND MY SUN NO LONGER RISE
REMEMBER WELL, MY LOVE FOR YOU
LIVES FOREVER, NEVER DIES!

***

The following collections of memories of early years on our hill farm in Chesterfield, Missouri, are presented as they were perceived and remembered by me. I realize that many events may have been overlooked or forgotten, and such events could be recalled in detail by other members of our family. I also realize that others may perceive the past events differently than I. It is hoped, that in reading this, my brothers and sisters will accept it in the context in which it is written. Such context is to provide a window for those of our families who come after us, through which they can see a bit of our life, as it existed in the 1930's and 1940's, enabling them to better understand our efforts, anxieties and our hope for their future.I give thanks to our God for the family into which I was born and for the family he gave me in marriage. I pray that we all succeed in our efforts to reach His Eternal Kingdom!

FOREWORD

Our paternal grandfather came from Bohemia, our paternal grandmother was of Scotch ancestry and our maternal grandparents from Germany. The maternal ancestors of our two half sisters were of Swiss origin. Our father, George J. Ruby, married Orlie Lugon about 1904. Two daughters, Hortense and Irene, were born, together with a son, George, who died from diphtheria when he was in the first grade. Hortense and Irene's mother died June 25, 1915 after which Pop and Mom (Mary A. Becker) were married. They took up residence .in Overland, St. Louis Co., Missouri. Eight children were born to Mom and Pop in Overland, beginning with Ferd and Joe (twins), Leonard (Boo), Jess, Mary, Bob, me and Tom. Jess died from pneumonia when he was two years old, only ten days before Mary was born. A mother never forgets her children and Jess's death was a sad memory all during Mom's life. She never ceased talking about "Little Jess" and how he died. Mom and the entire family had the whooping cough when Jess died and when Mary was born. In her weakened state, with the grief of her lost son, we can well imagine how difficult that time must have been for Mom and her new daughter.

Sis (Hortense) and Ed Musterman were married in September, 1924 and Irene and Wayne Kimler were married in 1928, the year before we moved to the hill farm in Chesterfield, Mo. The aforementioned is from history and not from my memory. What follows is of the years from 1929 as I remember them.

PART ONE
WILD HORSE CREEK AND THE 1930s

I peered down the hole into an incredible mass. My Christmas gift, a small metal hammer, was down there and could not be recovered. I was in the outhouse at our home in Overland, Missouri, and my hammer was where Mom had thrown it after I hit Huey Lee Hendrickson on the head with it. Mom was most unhappy with me but I couldn't understand why! After showing Huey Lee my hammer, he took it away from me and kept saying, "It's mine, its mine!" After I retrieved my gift, I promptly bashed his head in! It seemed the proper thing to do! Fortunately, Huey Lee recovered but when I visited him in California 18 years later, he still appeared to have a significant dent in his head.

This represents one of my earliest memories and, while hazy, another memory from Overland remains. Ferd and Mary were in the back yard with me and wouldn't let me go in the house. I wanted to see Mom but they said I couldn't because she was getting a new baby. Why would she be doing a thing like that? She already had a baby and that was me! She was probably still angry with me for hitting Huey Lee! Before the day was over, we had a beautiful new brother, his name would be Tom.

***

When Tom was only a few weeks old we moved to

Chesterfield. During the years of prohibition, the illegal manufacture of alcoholic beverages flourished. Pop was introduced to this practice by his brother Joe and some of his friends. The fact that it was illegal didn't seem to worry anyone, except Mom! She strongly objected when our basement in Overland was used to make what was then called "hootch!" After Pop and his friends enterprise was nearly discovered, Pop had decided that "city life" was not the way to raise a family with a bunch of boys, so he sold his excavating business to the Bostons and bought our 40 acre farm on Wild Horse Creek in Chesterfield. Uncle Bill Ziegler had owned the property and had built a rough shed for shelter when he was there. Pop, with the help of Ferd and Joe, built a two room addition to the shed before our move. The house would be ready when we arrived and the move was enthusiastically anticipated by Pop, Ferd, Joe and Boo. I could sense that Mom was sad, however, and couldn't understand it. I sensed that she was unhappy and hoped desperately that she would soon be happy again.

***

The house, our new home, was built on the crest of a high hill with a beautiful view for many miles. It probably was one of the highest points in that part of the county. The house was entered from a small porch on the Southwest side, then through a door which opened into the kitchen. On the right was our kitchen table, benches and chairs, with the wood cook range and cupboard on the opposite wall. Several rows of nails on the left side, as you entered, provided hanging places for coats and caps. A small table in the North corner held a water bucket, dipper and wash basin. Mom's flour barrel and a wood box stood to the left of the cook stove. One doorway opened from the kitchen to Mom and Pop's room and another door opened from the kitchen to the attached shed, which became our sleeping area. Mom and Pop's bedroom was the same size as the kitchen but had a small closet built into the North corner. A chimney between the two rooms provided a common flue for the cook range in the kitchen and a "warm morning" stove for the bedroom. A doorway to the shed sleeping area opened from Mom and Pop's room, also. The shed, to which the new addition was attached, was constructed of vertical boards and battens to which the battens were never applied. This left wide cracks for ventilation in both summer and winter. It was Pop's plan to remove the shed and finish the house as soon as money would become available. The house remained, as I have described it, for a long time, since the year was 1929 and we were entering a long, heartbreaking period of depression, the likes of which few had ever seen. There were two windows in the kitchen and two in the bedroom. The shed had a window in the South end and one was later installed in the North end. There were no glass panes in the window on the South. This window was covered with a piece of tin on which someone had practiced with a 22 rifle before it was retrieved for window duty. Pop always said that the Indians shot the holes through the window and there were some who believed him. The holes provided additional ventilation and sometimes a strange light pattern to the room.

***

The flat tarpaper covered roof, with the unfinished walls and ceiling, enabled the sleeping area to maintain the same temperature inside and outside, both summer and winter, with it being slightly warmer inside in the summer. Wind driven snow would create interesting little ridges on our bed covers during cold winter storms and rain always seemed to find a hole somewhere in the tar paper roof..

We had no electricity or gas and therefore the wood kitchen range provided any necessary heat and was the vehicle on and in which Mom created masterpieces of bread, coffee cakes, buns, mulligan, navy beans and many other goodies both winter and summer. Everyone ate fast in the kitchen in the summer so they could get outside in the sun to cool off..

Water was collected in a cistern at the corner of the house and was drawn by a leather strap with a snap attached to the water bucket. The leather strap also served a dual purpose in that it was used to correct boys who stepped out of line.

None of our family owned a tooth brush and, at that time, didn't know what one looked like. We cleaned our teeth using a clean cloth sprinkled with baking soda or a little salt. Kerosene lamps provided the necessary light for early morning and late evening chores. We generally went to bed early, especially in the winter, since Pop didn't want anyone to put wood on the fire in the kitchen range after 7:00 P.M.

Since we had no refrigeration, food needing to be kept cool were either stored in our root cellar or placed in a bucket which was then lowered by rope into the cistern, to hang just above the water. In later years we were able to get ice on occasion when the ice truck started to deliver to the Arbuckle farm. The truck driver refused to bring the ice up our hill, however, and we arranged to meet him at the bottom of the hill with a small wagon. We could then pull the wagon loaded with 50 or 100 pounds of ice up to the house.

The "root cellar" was dug into the sloping hill on the Southwest side of the house, was shored up with oak logs, was roofed over with oak logs and covered with earth. Canned fruit and vegetables were stored here, together with crocks of lard, potatoes, apples and root crops. The root cellar also served as a storm shelter where Mom would take us when severe weather threatened. She would herd us into the cellar, light a holy candle, and we would wait there until the storm danger had passed. If Pop were present, he would stand at the entrance to the cellar until the storm had reached us or had blown over. A heavy door was installed at the entrance, which, when closed would provide a safe, secure refuge from the weather. A second storm or "root cellar was later built near the South corner of our house. It was a bit larger and somewhat better constructed. The root cellar was also a cool favorite place for copperhead snakes and more than a few were found and eliminated there.

Mom washed all clothes by hand using water heated in a large iron kettle outside by the smokehouse. Pop always started a fire and heated the water for Mom early on each washday. Overalls were boiled with homemade lye soap and then scrubbed on a scrubbing board and rinsed. I still don't know how Mom could get everything done and still have time to help us with our problems. She baked 9 loaves of bread every other day, made coffee cake or cinnamon buns on Saturday for our Sunday breakfast and canned everything that would go into jars. She also sang in the choir at Ascension Church for the only mass which was at 7:00 A.M. Ascension Church was a mission church and was served by our pastor, Father McCartney, who lived at the principal parish at Centaur Station. Father had no means of transportation so someone with a vehicle from Chesterfield would go get him and take him back each Sunday. It was two miles to church, a long walk for little people but Mom always made it look easy and we always arrived well before mass began. It was only another 1/2 mile to Andy Kroger's general store by the railroad tracks in Chesterfield, so we generally walked there for any necessary purchases before starting home.

Apparently Pop and others in the family also sensed that

Mom was not happy. Ferd, Joe and Boo were always telling Mom about the beauty of the farm and described the creek through our property in glowing terms! "It's like a fairy garden, Mom," Ferd said one day, "you'll have to see it, wild flowers all over the banks and a crystal stream flowing through our property!" Pop was also urging Mom to allow him to take her to see the valley and the creek. I was hoping very much that Mom would agree to go since I was convinced that the spot must be beautiful and I wanted to see it also. Mom finally agreed to go. Pop had made a sled of oak runners and an oak deck. This sled could be pulled by our mules, Snowball and Red. This sled was often used to haul water from the creek. Two wooden barrels were tied to the sled and filled to the brim with the clear water from the creek. A piece of tarpaulin was tied around the top of the barrel to minimize the loss of water on the trip back up the hill. At best, about 2/3 of each barrel would survive the trip.

One pretty day, Pop hitched the two mules to the sled and Mom bundled Tom in her arms and sat on the sled with Mary and me next to her. I was filled with anticipation since we would soon see that wonderful fairy garden by the creek. A trail, which had been cut through the trees, led to the creek and descended at a steep grade. About halfway down the hill, the sled runner hit a small stump and Mom was thrown off with Tom still in her arms. Pop helped her back on and assured Mom that we were almost there. Mom was not happy and was adamant when she said, "Just take me back to the house, I don't want to see the place" My heart sank as we started back up the hill and it would be nearly a year before the older boys took me to the creek. It was many years before I really understood why Mom was unhappy with our move. We left a neighborhood where she had good friends, a house with electricity and running water and moved to a new area without any conveniences and a question of when, if ever, she may again enjoy even a simple luxury.

***

Our nearest neighbors were "Buck" and Lisa White, a black family, who lived in a little shack at the bottom of our hill, about 1/4 mile away. Mrs. White was a lovely little woman who always responded to a comment or statement with "Do Tell!" Buck seemed a bit strange and all of us kids steered clear of him. He would start yelling as you approached their place and Mrs. White would try to calm him down. He would yell, "Git off my place, this is my place now! Lisa you all come back here, I want them off my place, this is my place now!" Apparently Buck was not mentally far removed from the days of slavery and, although his home was but a shack, it apparently was the only place he could ever call his own. Pop often took potatoes and other vegetables down to them and we all wondered how they ever managed. Times were tough!

On one occasion I got to go to Chesterfield with Pop to pick up a sack of flour and some other things which were needed. It was shortly before Christmas and the weather was getting cold. Pop hitched the team to the hay frame wagon and I sat next to him on a board across the front. As we neared the White's house, Mrs. White came running down the hill toward us waving a handkerchief. Pop stopped and we waited. "You all goin to town, Mr. Ruby?" she asked. When Pop told her we were, she handed him a dime and asked, "We just don't have a thing in the house and if you all will just get me a dimes worth of corn meal, I'd be so much obliged!" Pop took her dime and we drove to Andy Kroger's store to get our supplies. Mrs. White was watching for us when we returned and met us at the bottom of her hill. Pop gave her the corn meal and then unloaded flour, some sugar and a slab of bacon. Mrs. White was shocked as she said, "Lordy man, I can't pay for all this, I only had that one dime!" Pop told her that there was no charge and he didn't want anything. Mrs. White put her handkerchief to her eyes but I could see the tears run down her black cheeks. She cried as she said, "Lordy man, how can I ever thank you, God Bless you, man!" Pop just waved and we drove on up the hill to our house. I sure liked Mrs. White!

Our other neighbors were the Steiners, whose farm was just over the hill northeast of the White's place. They had some dairy cows and sold milk and cream in town. Mr. and Mrs. Steiner had four sons, Oscar, Cliff, Roy and Harry. They also had a daughter, Berniece. Mrs. Steiner was hard of hearing, would cup her hand behind her ear, and respond to a comment with, "I declare!" Each neighbor seemed to have their own response, such as, "You don't say!", "Mercy!", "I declare!", "Pshaw!" and "Do tell!"

The hill lying to the East of our farm was owned by Dr. Arbuckle and usually occupied by tenants. A one acre piece was cut out of the Arbuckle hill and owned by Mr. and Mrs. Warwick Harman. Mrs. Harman called her husband, "Wart". I always thought that didn't sound very nice but he was of small size and didn't seem to mind the name. They had one daughter named, Dorothy Ann. The Harmans only came to their place on weekends or sometimes for short periods during the summer.

A bachelor, Andy Griffin, lived in a little two room cottage near the end of our land close to Wild Horse Creek Road. Across from his place was a small Negro settlement of the Jack Johnson families and Mr. and Mrs. Jefferson. A one room school house for Negro children was also located in this settlement, about 50 yards from the creek bank. Access to the school, the Johnsons and Jeffersons was from Wild Horse Creek Road.

About one mile north of our farm was a farm owned by Mr. and Mrs. Tony Reuther, located on Wild Horse Creek Road and almost across from our school house, Chesterfield Grade School #26. The Reuthers had three sons, Lawrence, Johnny and Eddy. They also had two daughters, Frieda and Bernadette. Mrs. Reuther was a jolly, fat lady who laughed easily and when she laughed she would hold both hands on her belly. We always tried to say something which would make her laugh so we could see her belly bounce and watch her glasses slide down her nose.

In a wooded area east of the Arbuckle house, and on their farm, lived a black family named Hawkins. This was a strange family of Mr. and Mrs. Hawkins and their seven children. They lived in a one room shack with a sleeping loft above. They were very shy and primitive. They carried their water in one gallon Karo syrup buckets, from a spring at the end of our lane at Wild Horse Creek Road. When they thought no one was within hearing distance they spoke in a language that no one else could understand. It probably was their original African native tongue. Pop said he heard what sounded like their language from a group which was brought to St. Louis for the 1904 world's fair. I know of no one who ever entered their shack and I'm sure no one ever wanted to go in there. Mrs. Hawkins would run from the shack when, on rare occasions, it was necessary to go by their house. She would run to the woods, hide behind a tree and peer around it until we were out of the area. The whole family was pretty spooky! A few years later the children were forced to attend the black school by the creek and I will describe some incidents, in relation to their schooling later.

The property which adjoined our farm on the Southeast was mostly heavily wooded and owned by Mr. Schneider. It was later owned by Mr. and Mrs. Harry Haeussler and their two sons, Harry and Ed. The Haeusslers became a very important part of our lives and knowing them was a bright spot in the gloomy years of the mid and late 1930's.

***

When Ferd and Joe returned from their first day in our new school, Pop asked where Boo was. Ferd said some kids were beating up on him! "And you left him?" Pop shouted! Pop said if any of our family needed help and they left without helping, they had better not even come home! The next day Ferd and Joe caught the molesters, held them down and stuffed horse manure in their mouth! He told them if they ever harmed any of the Ruby family, they would have to digest more than a little horse manure! All incidents stopped!

***

In the spring of 1930 Joe and Ferd started breaking new ground and Boo and Pop were busy clearing. The ground was mostly clay with a lot of roots and snags left from clearing. This made plowing quite difficult and, therefore, necessary that one person hold the plow and the other drove the team. It was on the occasion that Joe and Ferd were plowing a small patch southeast of our house that Boo took Tom and me out to watch. Tom and I were fascinated by the new turned earth and found our way into a new furrow. I saw the mules coming with Snowball walking in the furrow. I got out of the way! Joe and Ferd, intent on their chore, didn't see Tom in the furrow and Snowball stepped wide outside the furrow so she wouldn't step on him. The result was a wide furrow with Tom plowed under! Only Tom's foot was left sticking out. Ferd frantically dug him out and tried to get the dirt out of his eyes, ears, nose and mouth, then ran with him to the house. No injury or damage done but just a bad scare for all concerned! I never did understand why Tom kept his eyes upon while being plowed under! This incident restricted our movements for a time and limited our range from the house.

Later in 1930, Uncle Bill Ziegler came out to the house to see about some money we owed him. It seems we bought the mules, harness and wagon from him with the promise to pay him within the year. Since we had no money, he wanted his mules and gear back.. I remember his visit well. Not because of what Uncle Bill wanted but from watching him eat. Mom asked him to have lunch with us and he said he would have a cup of coffee but he had brought his own sandwiches. The sandwiches which he brought were jelly sandwiches, which was fine since we generally had jelly sandwiches for lunch. When Uncle Bill would take a bite of his jelly sandwich he would leave chewing tobacco stains around the bite on the bread! I was fascinated since it didn't take much, at that time, to interest me. I thought he would pinch that part off before taking another bite but he didn't. I was glad when he left!

Ferd and Joe hitched the mules to the wagon and drove them to Overland later that year. This left us with no means to farm our little crops! It was then that Uncle Gus Becker (Mom's brother) gave us a horse named Frank. He also gave us a wagon and a set of harness. Pop the found a mule (Jack) owned by Mr. Kort, of Chesterfield, and bought the mule for $25.00. We were back in business!

***

Thank the Lord for the good relatives like Uncle Gus

and especially Uncle Bill Abram. Uncle Bill Abram came out one day in 1930 or 1931 with a truck loaded with lumber and a whole crew of workmen. They built a new barn for us in one day! It was built to the East of the house by a red gravel pit. Uncle Bill knew that we had no money and he expected nothing for his most generous help.

***

On occasion, when Pop went into the village of Chesterfield for supplies, some of the local residents would approach him and ask, "How the devil do you make a living for you and your seven children on that old rocky hill farm?" Pop liked to lead them on and would smile and say, "All you need is a little corn and imagination and the money just rolls in!" They took him seriously and the story spread that Pop was making illegal liquor in our new barn. Someone decided to investigate during the night, and later said that his lantern was shot out of his hand when he was creeping toward our barn! The story was not true, at least no one shot out his lantern! If he was there, he probably caught the lantern on a branch, breaking the globe, and panicked, truly believing his own story. When asked about it, Pop would only grin and say he knew nothing about it. The story persisted for quite a while and no one approached our hill farm at night for along time.

***

In 1931 Uncle Bill brought a 1919 Model T. Ford sedan out to the farm and gave it to us! This was a gift of luxury which we could hardly believe! Buying the license and putting gasoline in the Model T restricted our use, however, for a number of months each year.

It was an incident related to this Model T that. I received

a most devastating and long lasting experience! I relate it here, not to discredit Pop for I loved and respected him very much. I tell of the incident to provide a lesson to all parents in dealing with their children, even in depressing and difficult times! It was a rare treat to go to the village in Chesterfield. There were several stores there with candy in their showcases and other people to see and listen to them talk. One day I heard Pop and Mom talking about the necessity of Pop going to the store to get a few things which also meant stopping at Mr. Biehle's for gas and some kerosene. Mr. Biehle was also a barber and had a small convenience store. There had been a few times that he had given us each a penny candy when we stopped there. I sure wanted to go along with Pop and asked him if I could. He looked at me for a few seconds and said, "You can't go with me, you're dirty! Look at your clothes!" I took this to mean that if I were clean, I could probably go. While Pop was busy getting ready to go, I washed my face and hands and put on a clean shirt and pants. It was summer and none of us wore shoes in the summer, except the older boys working the fields. I then quickly ran to the Model T and sat down on the passenger side. When Pop came, he opened the door, looked at me briefly, and said, "Where do you think you are going?" I said, "I'm going to the store with you, Pop." He said, "I told you that you couldn't go!" I answered, "Pop, you said I was dirty, look how clean I am!" With that, he closed the door and walked away as I figured that all was ok and I won my trip to the store. I watched Pop walk to where he had some sassafras tomato sticks stacked where he picked one up. I wondered why he would be taking a sassafras tomato stick to the village with us. He came back to the Ford, opened the door and jerked me out! He then knocked me down with the stick and started beating me across the back.. The Model T was parked next to a sloping terrace where Mom had planted some pink rambling roses. I was trying to crawl through the rose briars up the bank to get away but the blows kept coming on my back and legs! I then saw Mom running toward us from the house and she yelled, "George, why don't you just kill the boy!" Pop then stopped, turned away and said, "I might as well kill him, he's no goddam good, anyway!" I ran! I climbed into the hayloft of the old barn, hid deep in the hay, and cried. The pain in my legs and back from the blows were nothing compared to the pain in my heart! I had difficulty breathing and a lump seemed to rise in my throat and wouldn't go down! Pop said that I was no "goddam good" and he might as well kill me! I ran away! I went down the trail to the creek, and followed the creek nearly to Kehrs Mill Road before I sat down to think.. I had no place to run, no money, no clothes and most of all, I was afraid of the dark. I started back home but I knew that someday, somehow, I would leave all that I loved so much! I had to prove to Pop that I was worth something! The scars of that incident were with me a long time! It was not until I had children of my own that I realized how depressing those times must have been for Pop, having a large family, no money, no place to earn any, and to have a little kid with his nose to a candy counter hoping for a penny candy! Many years later, I'm certain that Pop was very proud of all his children, including me.

**

One Sunday Aunt Pauline came to the farm and invited us all to come to their club house on the Big River, near Cedar Hill, for the following weekend. Aunt Pauline said that she and Uncle Bill would have plenty of food, soda pop and beer and we could swim, fish and have fun. It sure sounded exciting and we were all hoping that we would go. Mom prepared for the next weekend and all nine of us packed into the Model T Sedan early on Saturday morning and pushed off the hill. The distance to Cedar Hill from Chesterfield was not very far but that trip was equal to a wagon trip over the Great Divide! It seemed to take forever since we encountered numerous detours and thirteen flat tire on the round trip. It was afternoon when we arrived at the club. They were glad to see us and the food and soda was mighty good! The older boys went swimming with Cousin Bill and it was fun to watch Bill dive off their dock. They encouraged Mom to go swimming and to take Mary, Bob and me with her. Aunt Pauline would take care of Tom. They would take us in a boat across the river to a sand bar where the water was only a few feet deep. Mom agreed that we would go. I was holding Mom's hand as we stood in the shallow water on the sand bar and watched the water go drifting by. Suddenly Mom just fell over and sank beneath the water! We couldn't imagine what was happening! She finally pulled herself up, telling us later that she became dizzy watching the current and seemed to lose her balance. While under the water, she saw a stick which she caught and used to pull herself to the surface. That incident ended our swimming as Mom demanded that we be taken back to the cabin. She never went wading again! The final trip home was a nightmare with more flat tires, detours and headlights failing on the Model T. Mom's prayers countered Pop's cussing and we finally made it home!

***

One day in 1931, Uncle Joe Ruby, (one of Pop's brothers) drove out to the farm in his wagon pulled by his horse, "King". Uncle Joe lived in Elmwood, St. Louis County, and we were surprised at the long distance which he drove his horse. Uncle

Joe wanted some potatoes and onions. He told us that he didn't have long to live and when he died he wanted Joe and Ferd to have his wagon and his horse, "King". He died about six months later! After his funeral, we went to his house and found the wagon. It had been damaged when it was struck by an auto some months earlier, but we got it home, along with old King. King died about six months after we got him. His carcass lay at the bottom of the hill below our new barn since it was winter and we had no way to bury him. Ferd was showing Harry Steiner the dead horse, which by then was badly bloated. Harry commented about how puffed up the horse looked so Ferd borrowed Harry's pocket knife and punctured the carcass. The escaping gas caused a rapid retreat and an angry Harry, who didn't want to use his knife again. By spring the carcass was nearly all devoured by wild scavengers, working from the inside out.

***

School sounded exciting and I looked forward to attending. I could watch from Mom's bedroom window for the older kids to return from school. They described the blackboards, chalk and books, all of which was new and interesting to me. I had attended a special introductory day during the Easter season which the school provided for those who would begin the first grade in August. This event was a party environment and families sent jello, cakes and cookies! I could handle a lot of that! Actual school that fall was quite different but we were fortunate in having a great teacher, Mrs. Jessie Schroeder, whom we all called, Miss Jessie. The school had between 40 and 50 students and was divided into two rooms. It was actually one large room separated by folding doors. Two small rooms off the main class room provided an area to hang our coats on racks and place our lunches on a long shelf above the racks. These rooms were referred to as the "cloak rooms". Cloaks were long out of style, no one used cloaks any more, but they continued to be the "cloak rooms". These rooms were also the area to which Miss Cuno, our other teacher and principal took students for punishment when needed! Clyde Backus nearly had an ear pulled off during a punishment session in the "cloak room"! Miss Cuno was no one to cross and her threat of "cloak room" punishment was enough to keep most of us in line! The lunches stored in the cloak room gave the room an interesting smell. While our lunches were not very exciting, consisting mostly of strawberry jam on home made bread, some students (who had fathers regularly employed) would sometimes have bologna on bought bread, bananas and even oranges. We were somewhat envious and I occasionally offered 1/2 of my jam sandwich to Bob Spaulding for his orange peelings. He never took the jam sandwich but always gave me the orange peel. The citron was different and I liked it.

***

Two of Mrs. White's grandchildren came to live with them, providing us with new friends to talk to and visit with at the bottom of our hill. Billy White was about my age and his sister, Emma, was about a year younger. Billy taught us to make toys out of buttons and out of wooden spools, on which sewing thread had been wrapped. He also showed me how easy it was to tattoo initials onto your arm. He had a neat "B.W." etched on his left forearm. I was interested! He took a willow branch, sharpened one end then scratched until the outer surface of skin was removed, leaving the scratched letters showing. I tried over several days and succeeded in getting a darn sore, scratched arm but no initials. I told Billy that he had the advantage since he only had to scratch the black off! Billy and I wrestled on occasion but he always won! As he would proceed to pin me, he would always say, "Raymond, I can whup you!" His nose ran a lot and I didn't relish being pinned beneath a dripping nose, so I always promptly gave up!

Mary and I delivered some vegetables to Mrs. White one warm spring day and Billy and Emma wanted us to stay and play. Since Mrs. White always wanted to remove a tip from Mary's ear, Mary wanted no part of sticking around any longer than necessary so she went home and I stayed. Mary had an extra little tip on one ear (it seemed to be a Ruby or Becker trait) and Mrs. White felt confident that it was simple matter to cut it off but we never found out if her method would have been successful. I guess I don't blame Mary! When Mary left, Emma White asked me if I would go swimming with her. I commented that there was no place to go to swim, so she pointed to a "hogshead" at the edge of the house. A "hogshead" is like a large wooden barrel sawed in half. The Whites used this to collect rain water from their house. Emma suggested that we swim in the "hogshead". That sounded like a good idea but I didn't want to get my clothes wet. "Take 'em off!" she directed. We both did just that and took the splash. Something was very different about Emma; she obviously was missing some various parts of equipment! I had no comment but remembered the kids at school who chided me about playing with black friends. When I asked why, they just said that black people were different! I guessed that the kids at school were correct! We didn't get to splash in that "hogshead" very long because Mrs. White came rushing out of her house, jerked Emma out of the water, spanked her and sent her into the house. I was next and she jerked me out, shook me and said, "You get your clothes on, Boy, and run home and tell your

Momma what you did!" I quickly dressed and ran up the hill, crying! I would tell Momma what I did if I only knew what it was! I described the event to Mom, as best I could. I expected sympathy but I got a whipping. Mom told me to never do that again! I promised and have never since gone swimming naked with a black girl!

In the summer of 1932, Aunt Annie came out to visit and invited me to stay with them for several weeks. She had made this offer to the others before, but the boys were unwilling to go. It sounded different and exciting to me, so I went with them. The city was a strange place to me with many strange people but it was exciting and, while I was somewhat fearful, I enjoyed it. During this stay, a near tragic event occurred at home. It was the practice for all of the neighbors to work together on major projects such as threshing during harvest, apple butter making and butchering during the winter months. The threshing run would begin as soon as the grain was ripe and move from farm to farm until the harvest was completed. This consisted of many team drawn wagons with drivers and loaders bringing the shocks of grain to the thresher and separator. The women and girls would prepare large amounts of food and assist in serving the working crews. We didn't raise oats or wheat on our hill farm but we assisted the Steiners and some of the older boys worked the "runs". When the Steiner family had completed their threshing, Mrs. Steiner invited our family over to their farm for a treat of home made ice cream. All went except Boo, who wasn't feeling well. Upon their return home, all became seriously ill and Pop started walking to Tony Reuther's for help. After realizing that Pop was already seriously ill when he left, Mom sent Boo to find him. It was fortunate that she did since Pop probably would not have made it! Dr. DeFoe was reached and he determined that they all had ptomaine poisoning, probably from something in the ice cream mixer, since all of the Steiners had the same illness. Fortunately, all recovered but it was a traumatic experience! Since I was at Aunt Annie's home, I escaped the unfortunate event. It was several weeks before everyone recovered.

For my return home, Aunt Annie bought me a new outfit with a white shirt and short white pants. When we reached the farm, Tom was glad to see me and he ran to me to put his arms around me. He had been playing in the dirt and was covered from head to toe! What a nasty thing I then did! I pushed Tom away saying, "Don't touch me, you're all dirty!" Mom was really furious and when Aunt Annie left, she treated me with contempt! I don't blame her I would have done the same! To make sure that I would not forget, Mom regularly reminded me and others of the incident over the next 15 or 20 years. A six year old should have known better and should not have been so easily influenced by a short stay in a more prosperous environment. I've always regretted the fact, that even for a moment, I would have thought that I was cleaner, had better clothes or was better in any way!

***

We attended Sunday mass and mass on holy days regularly and received our Christian training from Mom on an ongoing basis and from Father McCartney on Sundays after mass. In order to make our first communion, it was required that we complete the catechism instruction which was given by Father McCartney. We memorized all of the answers and completed the book with no problem but with no great understanding of the questions or answers! We then prepared for our first confession and I was quite concerned that I would do a good job of it. I reviewed all of the commandments and thought about each. The confessional was in a little room opposite the sacristy on the left side of the altar. Father sat behind a little slatted screen and the penitent knelt on the opposite side. My turn came and I entered. I could see through the screen and although Father rested his head in his hand, he could also see me out of the corner of his eyes. I made the proper preliminaries and then confessed the commandment which I had selected since it had a mature and mysterious sound to it. I told Father that I had committed adultery! He paused, peeked through the slats, and then asked if I was married. When I told him, "No", he said I couldn't have committed adultery since I wasn't married! Heck! The catechism lessons didn't say anything about being married so I guess I made a bad choice in selecting a commandment. There sure was a lot to know about this confession bit so I just thanked Father and left!

***

The depression was worsening and, in addition, a severe drought covered most of the mid west. This drought would last for several years, creating the great "dust bowl" in Kansas, Oklahoma, Nebraska and the Dakotas. The dry earth and strong winds created dust storms which reduced visibility to near zero in many areas. From high on our hill, we could often see the Western skies darkened as a result of these storms. Unusual weather patterns resulted, giving us scorching summers and bitter cold winters. Much of our crops burned up in the fields!

In spite of the depression and the severe conditions which were experienced daily, we often found things to laugh about. No doubt, some events should have been accepted with dignity and respect but we laughed any way. One such event occurred after Mom had all of her teeth pulled and was without dentures for a long time. We accepted the fact that Mom was without teeth and grew accustomed to her appearance. When Mom finally had someone to take her to Overland to see her dentist, and old friend, Dr. Dave Alben, she was determined to get the necessary dentures! She told the Doctor that she had to have some teeth but didn't have any money and didn't know how she would ever pay for them. Dr. Alben said, "Well Mary, why don't you just have the boys cut me a cord of wood when they can and get someone to deliver it to me?" Mom was delighted and she got her teeth. The Doctor also got that cord of wood and more later as he treated many of the family under the same terms. When Mom came home, she looked so funny with her new teeth we all just sat and laughed, when we should have complimented her!

***

The first crop each year was strawberries which we greatly depended on for necessary supplies to complete the year. Even during the depression years, strawberries brought good prices since produce shipped from great distances was generally not done at that time. Mom always bought a supply of sugar from the proceeds of first sales to assure her ability to "put up" the needed preserves, jellies, fruits and vegetables for the coming winter. Sugar cost $8.00 for 100 pounds and the first $8.00 went for that first sack. One summer, Mom canned over 800 quarts of jelly, fruits and vegetables. This was done on the old wood range cook stove but later we got a kerosene stove which could be used on the porch. Mom didn't care too much about the kerosene stove though, since she was a master at understanding and regulating the wood range. In addition to our first crop, we raised tomatoes, beans, sweet corn and all garden vegetables for market and our own use. We also had a large orchard of peaches, apples, pears and plums. Since the markets were primarily in downtown St. Louis, it was always a problem to get our produce there. For some time, a commission man made pickups in the village of Chesterfield and would take the produce to St. Louis where he would sell it for the best price he could get, deduct a commission of 10 cents per bushel, and deliver the net sales price to the producers. This worked fairly well, except for the fact that our produce brought the same price as inferior produce since it was generally sold in one lot. Pop always insisted that ours be the best and only quality produce was presented for sale. A new commission man began operating out of Gumbo and he promised better prices than what had been received. Pop decided to try him and he did provide better prices for the first few loads. After a short time, he disappeared, however, without paying for the last few loads delivered. I think Pop would have done him great harm if he could have found him. He settled for just labeling him a "no good sons a bitch!" Pop knew we needed a truck and regularly asked about for information on one which would be dependable and could be purchased at a reasonable price. He finally found a 1925 Model T in like new condition, which he purchased for $15.00. It was a great and exciting day when Pop, Ferd, Joe and Boo drove that Model T up the hill to our farm. Since our hill was quite steep, it was often necessary to come up the hill in reverse since the Model T had only gravity flow fuel system from the under seat tank to the engine. We later discovered that, by placing the nozzle of the tire pump on the vent to the gasoline tank and pumping vigorously, we could force air pressure into the tank and make the hill in forward low gear The truck opened a new world for us and we could soon take our produce to the market in St. Louis at 3rd street or at Sarah and Laclede or peddle door to door in the Clayton area.

***

Entertainment for us, at this time, was primarily listening to Pop tell us stories. Many were true stories and some were quite questionable. Little time was left for story telling in the summer but on occasion we would sit on the cistern box in the evening listening to Pop as the whipporwills and night creatures provided their accompanying music. In the winter we had more time in the longer evenings and we looked forward to Pop telling when he was a boy, some about his family and often about ghosts! We would all sit around the kitchen table or sit on the floor beneath the coat rack and listen. Although we heard the stories many times, we never tired of them and were anxious to hear them again. Pop told about his older sister, Ada, who was pronounced dead from an illness now thought to be sleeping sickness, and was buried. That night Grandma Ruby could not sleep and insisted that Ada was alive and the grave must be uncovered. Although it was thought that this was the actions of a grieving mother, Grandma's insistence had them unearth Ada's casket, viewing a sight they would never forget! Ada had turned over in the casket and pulled out most of her hair! Grandma never fully recovered from that horrible event. I wanted to think that this had not happened to one of my aunts, and always tried to put the thought out of my mind!

He told about his sister, Josie, who was murdered and the person committing the crime was never found! She had crawled the last 1/4 mile to their house and was dead near the steps where they found her! She had been stabbed several times! They found where she had crawled to the pond, near the house, where she bathed her wounds.

He also told of his Uncle John, who drank heavily and was cruel to his wife, Mary. After Mary's death , Pop and one of his brothers were in the back of his Uncle John's wagon coming back late at night from a neighboring farm. Pop said the team suddenly shied and stepped quickly to the left. A ghostly figure drifted past the horses, stopped opposite his Uncle John and looked up into his face! He gasped, "My God, it's Mary!" I don't know if this was true or not but Pop convinced us that it was.

Pop told of working the clay mines, of riding the rails south to Louisiana and of being stabbed in his side when he interrupted a fight on a trolley car in St. Louis. Bleeding badly as he jumped from the trolley, he made his way to an old barn where he found only cobwebs which he stuffed in his side to stop the bleeding. When he finally reached a doctor, he had the wound closed with stitches only to nearly die a few days later from infection! The doctor had neglected to remove all of the cobwebs! It was then opened cleaned and stitched closed again.

He told of seeing the great Hunkpapa Sioux Chief, Sitting Bull, when he was in St. Louis and would describe the "Battle of the Little Big Horn" to us in some great detail as it was told to him by those living at the time of the massacre. I think he may have been mistaken about seeing Sitting Bull, however, since the great chief was murdered in 1890 and Pop would have been only about 5 years old at the time of Sitting Bull's death. I think Pop saw Chief Red Fox, an Ogalala Sioux, who traveled with Buffalo Bill and made several appearances in St. Louis.

Pop had numerous ghost stories and had a way of telling them that would make your hair bristle and give you goose bumps the size of peas! He warned of certain paths at night where, he said a "Little Old Woman" would drop out of the trees onto your back and cackle gleefully while she rode on your back until you could shake her off! It seemed that all the paths or roadways, containing this danger, originated in the vicinity of our farm! He told us that old orchards were the worst places for the "Little Old Woman" and all of our short cuts happened to be through old orchards!

***

About this time, Union Electric started stringing lines along Wild Horse Creek Road and some of the first to hook on were the school and the Reuther farm. Electric lights suspended from the ceiling in the school building now replaced the kerosene lamps with reflectors which hung on the walls of the school rooms. The Reuthers had a single light bulb suspended from the center of the ceiling in their kitchen and living room. We were envious! A telephone line was then strung on the electric poles and a crank telephone was installed in the school. This became an information point for messages coming into the area. The Reuther family soon bought a radio and was the envy of many farm students in our school! They invited us to come over on Friday night to listen to a program called "Gang Busters". This program was based on actual gangsters and the efforts of the "G Men" in bringing them to justice. We didn't go to listen to the program very often, since it meant walking home in the dark through that same damned orchard where Pop said the "Little Old Woman" hid in the trees. The only way I could keep up, on the way home, was to lock my hands firmly into Joe's rear pants pockets. Joe said he didn't believe in the "Little Old Woman" story, but if she had been there, she would have had to jump mighty fast to land on Joe's back! He moved mighty fast through the old orchard!

Electricity would not be available to our farm until after World War Two. We continued with our kerosene lamps and lanterns. Someone gave us an Alladin kerosene lamp which used a mantle and gave a brilliant light. We were impressed! Since being exposed to the radio at the Reuther's farm, we longed for the day when we may have this luxury. It would come years later as a gift to Ferd and Joe from Mrs. Haeussler.

***

Mom seemed indestructible and we could not envision existence without her! It seemed that she was always doing something for us. She would be baking, cooking and washing clothes, ironing, making or mending clothes, helping with our homework and outdoor chores while encouraging everyone that "times would get better". One day, however, Mom faltered, looked pale and seemed very weak! After a few days she could no longer get out of bed and we were terrified! The weather was hot and the house was even hotter! Pop and the older boys would carry Mom outside and place her on a quilt beneath a tree on the Southeast side of the house. Mary, Bob and I would take turns fanning Mom and placing cool cloths on her head. Pop got Dr. DeFoe to come to the farm and he told us that Mom had malaria. He gave us some medicine and told us that Mom was very ill! We would all pray! Mary probably was the best at praying! We later learned Mary didn't want the rest of the family to see how worried she was and how often she was praying, so she went to the outhouse to pray! We feared that Mary was coming down with something also since she was making so many trips to the outhouse! I'm certain that the Lord didn't mind where the prayers originated since Mom recovered but remained weak for a long time. Mary assumed the role of cook, baker and housekeeper. She did a great job but I don't think she received any compliments. She did receive some comments that her bread didn't taste like Mom's!

***

The depression continued but now there was increasing talk that "next year" would be different. President Franklin D. Roosevelt was now in office a year since defeating Herbert Hoover and he promised a "New Deal". Somehow, in my mind, I thought that the next year "being better" had something to do with even and odd years. 1933 always had a negative, non promising sound to it but 1934 seemed to be the even numbered year when great things were going to happen! 1934 came and it was probably worse than 1933 since the summer was hotter and drier! The Roosevelt administration had implemented a number of programs, however, which provided hope and help to many in the poverty arena. The W P A and the N R A (National Relief Association) were approved and placed in motion. The emblem for the N R A contained an American eagle and, in itself seemed to instill some hope. We did not apply for relief since Pop and Mom felt that we'd just "make do" or "do without" until times got better. It was this year that Uncle Bill Abram came out one Sunday and scolded Mom for not getting some help under the provisions of the N R A. We needed clothing and coats and Uncle Bill said that they could be obtained without charge. Uncle Bill said he would come out the first part of the week and take Mom to Wellston to a J. C. Penny store where she could obtain some much needed items. He came out as promised and took Mom with him. They returned with socks, overalls and sheep lined coats for all of us. It was like Christmas in a very special way! This clothing and the clothing we got from city relatives provided covering for our bodies but our problem continued to be much needed shoes. Shoes were not necessary for most of us in the summer but were surely necessary in the winter! Rarely did anyone give us any used shoes. We always carefully maintained what shoes we had for long periods of time. When snow was on the ground, we would wrap our feet in burlap sack cloth and tie it with twine. (Plastics had not been invented yet) This always produced a strange sight when we reached school and, with others, unwrapped our feet!

One day, Tony Reuther told Pop that a friend of his had promised to get all the shoes he wanted. This friend was Mr. Vetter, a peddler who made regular visits, in his Model T. truck, to the Wild Horse Creek area. He said that he had access to new shoes which were salesmen samples and he would provide them free! We all wanted some! When the shoes arrived, we learned that they were all left shoes only and few of the same kind. Shoes were shoes though and, with some minor discomfort, we marched to school wearing two different styled shoes for left feet only. The tracks left in the mud on our lane to and from Wild Horse Creek Road were most unusual and would bring us to fits of laughter as we returned home from school.

***

Easter season was approaching and this was the year to introduce Tom to Chesterfield Grade School 26. He would start the first grade the next year and therefore would be a guest as we enjoyed our Easter special of jello, cookies and cake, an event that was much anticipated. We told Tom how nice it was and about all the good things we were going to get to eat. He was ready and anxious to go! When we arrived at school, however, the magnitude of 40 or 50 children, the teachers and all those goodies were apparently too much for him. He snapped! When Mary tried to quiet and comfort him unsuccessfully, Miss Jessie came to assist. It was a mistake! Tom unleashed a continuous barrage of all the cuss words he knew! "Doddam you, doddam this school, sons a bitch!" he shouted over and over! No words or assurances would quiet him. Mary suggested that we would have to take Tom home! I thought of bashing him in the head since I didn't want to miss the jello and cake. Good sense prevailed, however and we escorted Tom home without any of us enjoying the benefit of the goodies. I'm pleased to state that, upon entering first grade the following year, Tom became a model student and we eventually forgave his erratic behavior.

***

Since we were far removed from most of the families with children in our school, playmates were generally limited to school recess and since we had specific chores to do on Saturdays and non school days, little time was available for visiting. Sundays were generally non working days, however, and after mass, a variety of options were available for our Sunday afternoons. Mom often played cards with us on cold winter Sundays and she would always prepare a special Sunday dinner. We were often visited by relatives with Ed Musterman, Sis and family and Wayne and Irene being frequent visitors. We always looked forward to their visits. We greatly admired our brothers in law, Ed and Wayne, and always hated when it was time for the families to go home. Ed seemed capable of doing just about anything and I was always amazed at his skills. He was an excellent shot with a 22 rifle and always came back with squirrels when he went out. He was the only person I ever saw who could light a kitchen match with a 22 rifle at about 30 feet. He would stick the match in a fence post near the grape arbor and then fire the rifle so that the bullet would just graze the match head causing it to ignite! I later fired a lot of 22 rifle cartridges but never lit a match head. Ed could also catch fish when no one else could! If they weren't biting, he would go in the water for them using a method known as "hogging" or "fumbling" for fish. He would feel under logs and root snags and often come up with a fish. We never tried that for fear of putting our hands on a snake or in the mouth of a muskrat or mink.

***

During the summer of 1934, our nieces, Tudor and Shirley, came to visit and spent several weeks with us. Tudor was just a few months younger than I was and I looked forward to their visit. Pop made certain we didn't get too rested or too inclined to play so he promptly added Tudor to our hill farm work force. Pop firmly believed that all row crops should be hoed often and be kept weed free. He included our corn fields in that policy also and, while they were generally planted "in check" to be cross cultivated, the weeds still managed to sneak in there. We were always awed by the size of the fields and the rows where we couldn't see the other end. Pop always made it sound as though it was going to be fun with a promise that we could go swimming when we were finished. The constant thought of that cold, clear water in the creek kept us chopping and hoeing but it was never quite fun. Tudor's first encounter with a big field of corn and a sharp hoe caused her to question the promised swimming reward but we persevered. Shirley and Tom were still a little too short to handle the hoes but, while Shirley escaped a good part of hoeing chores, Tom later was introduced to Pop's sharp hoes and non ending rows of crops. Tom didn't like hoeing any more than Mary, Bob and I did! As a matter of fact, Tom disliked it so much and complained so vigorously that Bob and I took some pleasure in teasing him which seemed to make our chore somewhat easier. We would start to sing, "Hoe it down and chop that cotton,

Dixie Land is long forgotten". This seemed to make Tom even more distressed and we enjoyed it! It probably was a nasty thing to do! Pop would let Tudor and Shirley ride the horse and mule to the creek to be watered. Shirley seemed so small sitting on that large animal and her eyes seemed exceptionally large when the horse lowered his head to drink and Shirley feared that she would just slide off over the horses head! That year Sis delivered a new daughter. Our new niece was a round faced cutie who they named Mary. Sis later added son George, completing her family of four children.

***

The Harman family only came to their little cabin on week ends and attended mass with us. We always sat in the second pew on the right side of church and the Harmans would occupy the pew directly in front of us when they attended. One Sunday Mrs. Harman turned around, before mass began and gave Tom and me each 2 cents. We were delighted! This could provide something special from Mr. Biehle's store or Andy Kroger's store when we next arrived there! We promptly pocketed our wealth. Mrs. Harman glared at us as the collection basket moved past us. After mass, she strongly commented that the coins were for the collection basket! This seemed odd to me, since, if that was what she wanted to do with the four cents, why didn't she put them in the basket herself! Besides, Father McCartney probably received over a dollar in the basket as it was! Mrs. Harman was not pleased but we kept the coins.

A neighbor would occasionally invite Mary to come to their place on Sunday afternoon and visit with their daughter. I went with Mary one Sunday afternoon and listened to her friend describe the dancing lessons she was taking. She was wearing an outfit consisting of a blouse and a loose fitting pair of shorts with wide legs. As she demonstrated her dance, which included high leg kicks, an awful lot of her was exposed! I was embarrassed but I didn't leave! I later described the incident to Bob. "Bob, she shouldn't dance wearing clothes like that, you could even see her balls!" "Girls don't have balls!",Bob snapped! I was surprised, "They don't!" "Of course they don't!" Bob was getting irritated. Bob was pretty good about such things, but I didn't want to always be wrong, so I said, "Bob, maybe some of them do, cause I think this ones got 'em!" Bob walked away in disgust! Many years later I learned that Bob was right, as usual.

***

One day in 1934, several people on horseback emerged from the ridge road on the wooded acreage southeast of our house. They rode to the house and introduced themselves as Harry and Eddie Haeussler. Their family owned the acreage adjoining ours and planned to build onto the existing log cabin on their property. They were friendly, quite talkative and interesting. Mom invited them in for some home made bread and strawberry jam. They enjoyed the home made products and thanked Mom for it. Mrs. Haeussler visited us later and we found her also to be a most delightful person with a lot of energy and enthusiasm. Harry and his mother became our favorite visitors. We liked Eddie, but he always seemed to me to be aloof and looked down on the younger members of our family. Mom loved the compliments on her home made bread and coffee cake and Harry never refused to join us for a sample of her bakery skills. The Haeusslers became a bright spot in our lives of the 1930s and 1940s.

***

Wild Horse Creek Road was lightly traveled in the

1930s and all students of the Chesterfield Grade School #26 would turn from their lessons to watch out the window when a vehicle went by. Such vehicle might be Jim Corless driving his horse and buggy to town, a Model T truck or sedan or a Model A Ford. Miss Jessie's 1930 olive brown Model A was always parked directly in front of the school. She picked up several students who lived over near Strecker Road or Kehrs Mill Road. We were always envious of those students who got a ride to school on cold or rainy days. One day in 1935, we were excited when we saw a red 1934 Ford pick up truck pull up in front of the school. It had a name painted on the side which I had not heard or seen before, "Coca Cola". We assumed that a parent or relative of one of the students was ill or had died, since our school often became the message center for the community. The driver came to the school door and spoke briefly with Miss Cuno. He then went back to the truck and climbed onto the bed where there was a large red cooler with that same name on the side. Miss Cuno told us all to remain seated and quiet and that this man represented the Coca Cola Bottling Co. and they wished to give us each a sample bottle of their cold soda. We were absolutely thrilled that a company would do that for "free!" He brought several cases into the classroom and we each received a bottle of Coca Cola. It was the best tasting drink I had ever tasted! The man said that the soda cost 5 cents each so it was not likely that we would often afford another bottle. At our year end picnic, however, Coca Cola was available and each student was given five slips of paper worth 5 cents each which could be exchanged for anything being sold. With our new found wealth of 25 cents we could once again sample that great bottle of soda, along with juicy fruit gum or Mr. Goodbars, all of which were 5 cents each.

***

The drought continued, along with the depression and we continued to "make do" or "do without". We were all happy together and I dearly loved and admired each member of our family. Apparently Mom had now accepted and adjusted to life on our hill farm. She still sang the same songs as she washed clothes, however, but somehow they seemed less sad. The songs were, "If I Had the Wings of an Angel, O'er These Prison Walls I Would Fly!" and "The Death of Poor Floyd Collins".

Our summer days began in the early dawn and Pop continued to make the field chores sound as though they were going to be great fun. His regular instructions continued to be, "We'll get our hoes good and sharp and start in the cool of the morning, then come the heat of the day, we'll stop and you can go swimming". When we looked at the seemingly endless rows of corn, our enthusiasm quickly waned. We would generally quit at noon, however, and after lunch we would water the cows at the creek, stake them out to graze and then swim in the icy cold spring water of the creek. Those were great and enjoyable times (the swimming part). We always looked forward to the times when Mary would accompany us on early morning blackberry picking trips. We would laugh, joke and race to see who could fill their pail first. We always went swimming following blackberry picking since we had to wash the "chiggers" off. I don't know if that helped, but we thought it did.

We had two pet, brightly colored pigeons named, "Maggie" and "Jiggs". They were beautiful birds, would come to our call and were especially fond of Mom. On wash days they would sit on her shoulder and "coo" as Mom sang some of her favorite songs. They, along with our dog, Midget, were a part of our hilltop family. One day two hunters came to the farm and asked permission to hunt. Mom said OK and they went along the woods to the fields south of our house. They were gone no more than an hour when we heard shots fired and shortly thereafter they returned to their car. Bob and I ran to them to see what they got and they answered, "Nothing!" Bob saw the beautiful brightly colored feathers of one of our pigeons sticking out of the game pocket of one of the men's jacket! Maggie and Jiggs were gone, the hunters killed some members of our family and left quickly before we could tell Mom what they did! Mom was furious! Never again did we allow any strangers to hunt on our property or to hunt from our place!

The winters were bitter cold and it was good to be inside near the wood range. The outhouse, located about 100 feet to the north of our house, was especially cold! Somehow, in my young mind, I thought the seat would be warmer if someone used it first and I could follow quickly behind. It never was! The icy drafts that swept in from below would pucker the hardiest of rear ends! In the winter, it took us little time to go to the toilet!

Shortly before Washington's Birthday, in February of 1935, a sleet storm mixed with freezing rain covered the several inches of snow already on the ground. Most of Wild Horse Creek was frozen over with the exception of patches of faster flowing water and areas near a spring entrance. Often ducks would select these areas to settle overnight and feed during the day around shocks of corn still standing in adjacent fields. Since duck season was closed, we were surprised one day to hear a series of shotgun shots fired in the area of the creek. Pop decided to walk down the hill to see who did the shooting. While he attempted to walk quietly, the ice covered snow telegraphed the crunching noise created by his footsteps. It was Andy Griffin doing the shooting and he heard the crunching footsteps in the clear cold air. Thinking that a game warden would be checking the shots, Andy quickly circled through a field and woods and dropped by our house. He knocked on the porch door, opened the door, and tossed seven big mallard ducks on the floor. "Here, Mrs. Ruby, I want you to have these!" It was rare for Andy to give us any of his game, but Mom gladly accepted and thanked him, while inviting him in for a cup of coffee. Andy promptly declined and hurriedly left for home. Pop came in a few minutes after he left and asked where Andy was. Pop had recognized Andy's boot tracks. Mom told him the story and showed Pop the mallard ducks. Pop had a good laugh since he quickly saw that Andy didn't want to be caught with illegal game and decided the best out was to drop the ducks and the blame on us. Mom decided that we should invite Andy for a roast duck dinner on Washington's birth day, however, and he gladly accepted. We made him feel that his contribution of the ducks was very much appreciated and his generosity would long be remembered. Andy never knew that we suspected the truth in his action. During the dinner, Andy commented on how good the coffee was and Mom complained about the high cost of coffee. "Why, by gawd, my sister in St.Louis gets coffee for 10 cents a pound!" Andy advised. Mom said she just couldn't imagine getting coffee at that price and asked Andy if his sister could get her some. He said she surely could and he would tell her when he next wrote to her. Mom gave Andy $1.00 and said she would like to have 10 pounds. Andy delivered the coffee about a month later and it was the most disappointing coffee we had ever tasted! Mom guessed that it was about 90% chicory, 8% something else and 2% coffee. We used that supply up and never ordered any more!

***

Hogs were butchered in early winter when we were reasonably certain that the weather would remain cold. The filled smoke house gave us a good feeling when we looked at the hams, bacons and shoulders hanging or salted down. Pop also hickory smoked the sausage. Breakfast included fried bacon, hog jowl or ham with Karo syrup and home made biscuits. Mom could crank out a batch of biscuits in little time from the old wood range and they were just excellent with that syrup and smokehouse goodies. Mom often alternated with mush, oatmeal and pancakes. I've never been able to duplicate her pancakes, which were frying pan size and could be rolled up with jam or jelly inside.

***

During the winter, I awakened one morning and was terrified since I couldn't open my eyes. I was frightened as I called for Mom to help me! My eyes were sealed shut with matter from some kind of infection! Mom put me on a chair next to the stove and told me that she would take care of me as soon as she finished getting everyone else off to school or to work. As I sat there, in only my long winter underwear, I could envision what was taking place in the kitchen. I could smell the food and hear the bacon frying. Although Mom hurried to get to me, it seemed forever, in this new world of darkness! Mom bathed my eyes with warm water and unsealed the lashes. I now could see! This procedure was repeated each morning for more than a week since each night they would seal while I slept. My eyes were sore! Ed Musterman, Sis and family came out the following Sunday and Ed insisted that he take me to our neighbor, Dr. Arbuckle, who would likely be at his farm this weekend. Although Dr. Arbuckle was an ear, nose and throat specialist, he examined my eyes. I had "Pink

Eye!" I thought only cows got pink eye but I was wrong. Dr. Arbuckle gave Ed some medicine for my eyes and in a few days the problem disappeared. I was sure glad!

***

Entertainment, at that time in the country, was pretty much limited to what could be originated on your own. In addition to hunting, fishing and the usual outdoor games and activities, some forms of amusement took on a cruel, and sometimes, sadistic form. Teasing was one such form of amusement. One day Arthur Brierbauer drove to the house to discuss the wheat threshing plans. He owned the steam engine, thresher and separator, which he moved from farm to farm during the threshing "run". He had his young daughter, Kathleen, with him. I watched her all the time he visited, thought she was cute, but said nothing. When they left, Ferd asked me what I thought of Kathleen, and I said, "I couldn't keep my eyes off her!" That was a mistake! Ferd, Joe, and all the Steiner boys teased me about "Arter's daughter" and "Arter and his tresher". That is the way Mr. Brierbauer talked. This went on for a number of years and I hated poor Kathleen and rarely spoke to her during our school years at Chesterfield Grade School #26. When Arthur Brierbauer moved his steam engine and equipment, he would pass the school house on Wild Horse Creek Road. The steam engine moved very, very slowly and everyone, except me, watched the engine as it passed. I didn't want to watch for I feared that someone would accuse me of being too interested in "Arter's tresher!"

***

One cold Sunday, Roy, Cliff and Harry Steiner came over to go rabbit hunting with Joe and Ferd. I asked if I could go along to carry the rabbits. Some protested but they finally agreed that I could go. Roy Steiner seemed to speak up for me and I always felt that Roy was pretty much a friend and seemed considerate of the younger kids. When we reached Wild Horse Creek at the bottom of our hill, I realized that I would be unable to cross on the sycamore log spanning the stream. The creek had a coat of ice about 1/2 inch thick.. When I said I couldn't cross the log, Roy offered to carry me across. I appreciated his concern and was grateful for his offer. When we reached the middle of the log, however, he stopped, took me by the hands and held me over the ice. I thought he just wanted to scare me and I said, "Don't do that, Roy!" With that, he proceeded to bounce me up and down on the thin ice until it broke. He then lowered me into the icy water up to my waist, pulled me out and placed me back on the bank where we started! "You better run home fast now, before you freeze to death!" Roy shouted after me but I was already running! I was crushed! After changing into some dry clothes, I placed roofing nails under all four tires of their car! It seemed the proper thing to do! From incidents such as this, I developed a nasty temper, a combative attitude and would readily fight when provoked. Attempts to strike at the Steiner boys when they teased me would never produce results since they would simply grasp me by the shirt and hold me at arms length until I tired of swinging. I could never reach them but often dwelled on some method of doing so. I prayed for longer arms! They called me "Pop Eye" and would greet me with "Blow me down, Pop Eye" and then laugh because they knew I couldn't reach them. The eldest Steiner had a son named, Marvin, who was about six or seven years older than me. Marvin decided that he, also would take up the chant and I resented him more than the others for his teasing. Marvin was tall, heavy set and stupid! One day he came to our house when I was guarding a watermelon which we had cooling in a washtub of cistern water on the northwest side of the house. As Marvin approached, he pushed me on the shoulders, grinned and said, "Blow me down, Pop Eye!" Since I was standing slightly uphill from him, I felt that I could reach his head and promptly swung a hard right to his nose! Blood squirted everywhere and Marvin was terrified! He was yelling and half sobbing as Pop came around the house to see what the problem was and he told Pop that I hit him. Pop gave me a mild scolding, in which he didn't seem to have much heart. The teasing slacked off after that and stopped altogether by Marvin. All of the Steiners, including Marvin, are now deceased and I think of them often, but not unkindly.

The highlights of each year were the Christmas school play, the school picnic, the fourth of July when Uncle Phil, Aunt Annie and family, would come out to the farm with friends for a BBQ, apple butter cooking and hog butchering. The school Christmas play was presented by the students and we practiced diligently for our parts. Practice usually began about 30 days prior to the play and was presented in the school house. It was always well attended. The play was preceded by our own school band which consisted of Miss Jessie at the piano and nearly everyone else with some makeshift instrument. We did have drums, triangles and tambourines but the balance consisted of wooden sticks and blocks which were rubbed or hit together in keeping time with the music. Capes and hats were worn by the band, all of which were made by our parents. Our capes were blue with a gold flap and our hats were made from cut off oat meal boxes and covered with the same material. A band director was chosen from among the students and I had the opportunity to direct several times. I never thought the band sounded very good but the audience always clapped enthusiastically anyway. Santa Claus arrived after the play amidst a clatter of hooves or blowing horns and this represented the high point of the event. Santa gave each student and children in attendance a beautiful orange and a small package of hard candies. We cherished the gifts and would try to make the candies last as long as possible.

The school picnic was held at Rinkel's Grove in Bellefontaine (we called it Hilltown) during the month of May. School always closed about the 15th of May so that the farm students could help with the planting and spring chores. Each student was given 25 cents, in script, to spend as they wished at the school picnic which made this a great day and was always eagerly anticipated. Several students received $1.00 from their parents to spend at this picnic. We couldn't imagine anyone with that kind of money and then to spend it all in just one day! This year end school picnic always featured a play with students performing for parents, relatives and the community. For some reason, each play had a black character in the cast and it seemed that I was always selected to play that part. The plays always seemed to be appreciated by those attending, and, while I don't think they were very good, there just wasn't much of anything else available.

On the last day of school each year, Miss Jessie and Miss Cuno would award those students who had not missed a day of school and those who had not missed a word in spelling for the entire year. The award was a 25 cent box of chocolate covered cherries and was highly coveted by all. We rarely missed a day of school unless we were very sick. Weather never kept us from school and I remember Pop hitching the team to a drag and dragging to compact the snow from our hill to Wild Horse Greek Road, so that we could manage the walk better. One winter a student attended with swollen jaws and neck giving the appearance of a chipmunk enroute to his burrow with jaws stuffed with goodies. The student's name was LeRoy Whalen and his family lived 3 1/2 miles from school, meaning a daily 7 mile round trip walk for lessons. The teachers questioned LeRoy's appearance when he arrived, suggesting that he had the "mumps" and should return home. He strongly denied the "mumps", said his mother told him it was just swollen glands and that he was fine. He continued to come to school each day. In a short period of time a large percentage of students were home with the "mumps"! On the last day of school, LeRoy was the only student who had not missed a day and he proudly accepted his 25cent box of chocolate covered cherries! We hated him! It seemed a great price to pay for those cherries since most of us knew what careless treatment of "mumps" could do to boys. I don't imagine LeRoy ever fathered any children!

***

Traditionally, on the Fourth of July each year, Uncle Phil, Aunt Annie, their families and some close friends and neighbors, came to the farm for a picnic. They brought spare ribs, soda, beer and everything necessary for a great picnic. Pop built a large hickory fire early on that day so that the coals would be just right for the BBQ. Uncle Phil's next door neighbor, George Hoechst and family, always came with them. George was the designated chef and delighted in cooking the meat over those coals. He always had a steady delivery of cold beer coming to him to compensate for the heat. It seemed that George would be pretty well cooked before the BBQ was finished. He was funny when he had enough beers and we always enjoyed him. Uncle Phil often gave a dollar to each of us children to assure that everything would be cleaned up when the picnic was over. We were delighted with that kind of money!

Apple butter cooking and hog butchering was always done with the help of several neighbors and we also assisted them in these projects. These events always produced some of the best pies, cakes and goodies, since all the farm wives tried to present their very best. The dinner table was something to behold. The only problem I had with the butchering event related to cleaning the entrails for casings for stuffing sausages. This cleaning was done on the kitchen table and, while the table and area was always thoroughly cleaned before serving lunch, the slime and refuse from the entrails scraping left a rather unpleasant aroma in the kitchen. This aroma seemed to linger during meal time and took a little edge off the fantastic prepared spread. Home made grape wine always seemed to be available at butchering time and no one seemed to pay much attention to us as we moved back for seconds, thirds or fourths!

***

The flour barrel stood in the corner, next to the wood range and, directly behind the barrel was stored a hickory stick which Mom used to discipline boys who needed it. It seemed we often needed it and, on occasion, were punished for something we didn't do. Considering, however, the times we escaped punishment for something we did undetected, I think we came out on the plus side. I went through several days without a switching one time and was feeling mighty good about it, so I then did a very foolish thing! I went to the woods, cut a young hickory sapling, peeled the bark and proudly presented it to Mom. "What's this for?" she asked. I explained it was a switch for those other kids who didn't mind, since I was good! She took the switch and placed it behind the barrel. She didn't seem pleased!

Saturday was bath day, and that event was accomplished in a galvanized wash tub placed in Mom and Pop's room. Since water was always conserved, and never wasted, several baths were taken before the water was changed. It was always a privilege to get the first bath. The Saturday following my generous contribution of the new hickory switch, Bob and I argued about who would get in the tub first. We couldn't agree so we both stripped to see who would be first. At the tub, a fight erupted and suddenly, like a small tornado, Mom moved onto the scene and we both got a sampling of my new hickory switch on our bare bodies. I got it first! I sulked and dwelled on the fact that life didn't seem to be fair and also on how stupid a guy can be!

***

One morning we awakened to see smoke rising from the Haeussler's woods. Pop, Ferd, Joe and Boo left immediately to investigate! They didn't go far since Haeussler's woods were on fire and the fire was spreading with frightening speed. Pop and the boys hitched the team and plowed furrows around our fields bordering the woods. The fire increased with intensity and we could see the flames shooting high above the tree tops! The wind then increased and shooting sparks and embers were flying high in the air, with some landing in the area of our house. Mom gave Mary, Bob and me some wet sacks and sent us to the strawberry patch where we beat out the burning embers as they fell on the straw. We could not face the blazing woods due to the intense heat, even though the woods were about 1/4 mile from our house! We learned that a fire truck had been called in from Hilltown and promptly got stuck in the woods off Kehrs Mill Road. The truck would not have helped had it reached the fire, however, since the fire had covered over

100 acres. When all seemed pretty hopeless, it began to rain and the rain controlled the fire and eventually extinguished it. Several days later we walked through the burned woods and found dead birds and animals. Apparently the birds could not fly high enough to escape the heat. The smoldering logs and dead creatures left a sad picture in our minds.

***

Mom was always supportive of our school efforts and never interfered with any discipline the teachers imposed. That policy came near to being changed due to an event which forced Bob into a punishment which was similar to "being shunned" for an unreasonable length of time. We often walked as far as our lane with other students who lived on Wild Horse Creek Road. One such family who walked with us was the Glaser family. The eldest was Charlene and the next was Donald, who was in my class. Their Grandfather was president of the school board and Miss Cuno went the extra mile to keep him happy during his frequent stops at the school. It was not unusual for boys to make jokes about their teachers, even though we had a great regard for them both. During a walk home, one day, Bob told Donald

***

The Author, Ray Ruby, as a young boy growing up on the hill farm.

Pop with new litter of pigs. Our winter supply of hams,
shoulders, bacons and sausage. Our barn in the background
with chicken house on right.

Mom with Irene and grandson Wayne in sleigh, pulled by our horse, "Bill". On the hill farm in Chesterfield about 1936.

Our sister, Mary, ready for her first date.

Irene (left) and Hortense (sis) stirring apple butter. Many bushels of apple butter were cooked each year for our winters supply.

Pop, an expert woodsman, could drop a tree within a foot of the planned fall. The crosscut saw built muscle and character for growing boys.

Our parents, George and Mary Ruby, (Pop and Mom) at our farm on Wild Horse Creek in Chesterfield, Mo.

Left to right – Ray, Tom, Mary, Ferd (holding Wayne), Bob. Back row – Leonard (Boo), Joe and Pop. On the cistern box at our house on the hill.

The Ruby children -1986 - Standing-back row, Tom Irene,
Ferd, Sis, Bob and Mary. Kneeling- Joe and Ray. At Joe's
farm in Farmington, Mo.

what to do if Miss Jessie tried to hit him. Bob said he should kick her in the shins and when she stooped over to rub her shins, he should kick her in the rear. Donald told Charlene who promptly told her father and mother, who promptly told the Grandfather who took the matter to the teachers. Bob was called into see Miss Cuno privately. Bob explained that he was just making a joke but that didn't satisfy Miss Cuno. After berating Bob for his comment, Miss Cuno instructed all of the students, including us, to avoid Bob and have no conversation with him. We, of course, ignored her directive but most of the students followed her orders. Mom didn't seem to mind the punishment for the first day, but when the penance continued into the third day, Mary complained bitterly to Mom. That did it! Mary delivered Mom's message to Miss Cuno the following day, "If Bob's punishment was not eliminated that day Mom would visit the school to "DISCUSS THE SEVERITY OF HIS PUNISHMENT"! Bob's penance ended that day and we had very guarded conversations with the Glaser family after that episode.

***

We continued to haul our produce to market in St. Louis at the Sarah and Laclede or 3rd Street Markets. We would leave the farm at midnight and arrive at the stands between 3:30 and 4:00. in the morning. I often accompanied Pop and would help him sell produce from the truck. The trip from home seemed strange at first. The valleys would be quite cool and I often wore my sheep lined coat. We drove down Olive Street Road all the way to the city and would rarely see a light until we reached the Imperial gas station just West of Woodson Road on Olive Street. Pop nearly always stopped there for a little gasoline and a pack of "Bull Durham" tobacco. Gas was 15cents a gallon and the tobacco was 5cents a sack which included the cigarette papers. When we reached the city, we would see many people sitting on their porch or front steps. At 3:00 AM this seemed quite odd to me but it was just too hot to sleep in the city. Air-conditioned homes were unknown at that time and even if they were available, few could have afforded one. At the market, I would watch poor black women scavenge for discarded cabbage leaves, lettuce leaves, turnips, tomatoes, potatoes and what ever else they could find. They poked through the garbage cans until they had their sack filled with something that could be turned into a meal for that day.

Uncle Bill Becker frequently brought produce to the market and it was always great to see him and watch the twinkle in his eyes as he talked. He would always take me to a little restaurant across from the market stalls, and buy us each a hamburger and a cup of coffee. Those hamburgers cost 10 cents and the coffee was 5 cents, some of the best I had ever eaten. If we were not successful in selling all the produce, we would return by way of Clayton or Overland and try to peddle the balance door to door. Usually, this was successful but on occasion we would deliver the balance to the Little Sisters of The Poor. There were times that an offer for each bushel of tomatoes would not even recover our cost of 15 cents for the empty box.

One summer, a buyer told Pop that there was a great demand for winter onion sets and they would sell fast. That was good news, for we had a large patch of winter onions. It would only be a matter of plucking, separating and drying the sets. We picked onion tops and carried sacks of them to the loft in our new barn. Sis came out and helped us separate the clusters into individual sets. It was a long, hot chore that was made a little easier as we sang songs and told stories. We wound up with several burlap sacks filled with onion sets. It would be a real bonus and would probably mean new shoes for all of us. When Pop took them to the market, no one wanted any and they couldn't be sold or even given away! On his return home, he dumped the sacks in the ditch alongside our road going up the hill to our house. The sacks served as a water break and, every spring thereafter fresh winter onions would shoot up from the ditch. Unhappy memories returned as we came home from school and saw the onions, recalling the hot loft, the long days and the wasted effort!

***

One day, a man named Mr. Wilson, who lived somewhere West of Kehrs Mill Road, drove up the hill to our house. He had a long handlebar mustache and was driving a Model T Roadster. I don't know what his first name was but for years we referred to him as "Handlebar Wilson". He wanted to get some tomato and cabbage plants. While Pop was getting the plants, we talked, or rather listened, to Handlebar. We asked him about some of his travels and he told us that he had been to Oklahoma, Kansas, Iowa and Minnesota. All of those places seemed a long way from us. He told us that he specifically went to Stillwater, Oklahoma to see Cole Younger, who was a life prisoner there. Cole Younger and his two brothers rode with Jessie and Frank James. Cole Younger and his two brothers were shot, wounded and captured while trying to rob the bank in Northfield, Minnesota. Jessie and Frank James escaped! A group of farmers and business men, armed with shotguns and rifles, were waiting for the gang when they arrived in the town! It was the last big robbery for the James gang! Cole Younger was wounded eleven times but lived to serve out his sentence!

"Handlebar" said that Cole was surly and only talked a little when he gave him some tobacco. "Handlebar" was interesting and we wished he could have stayed longer. When he got the plants and prepared to leave, we were surprised at the method he used to start his roadster. He cranked the Ford several times, then got in and turned the key on. It started! We had never seen anything like that and I still don't know how it worked. He then wheeled the Ford around by cutting up over a bank and headed down the hill. In addition to being a good talker, "Handlebar" was a wild driver! "Handlebar's" visit brought to mind "The Ballad of Cole Younger" which we had often heard. I don't remember all of it, but the song tells of a dream by Bob Younger, in which he saw the abortive raid on the Northfield bank by the James gang, and tried to warn his brother, Cole. Part of the song went something like this: "Now brother Bob did say, Cole, if you undertake that job, you'll surely curse the day! But I stationed up my pickets, and away to the bank I flew, and there, upon the counter, sir, I struck my fatal blow! The robbing of the Northfield bank, I know I can't deny, and now I am a prisoner, in the Stillwater jail I lie!"

The winter of 1934-35 was very cold and we looked forward to spring. Each Saturday or school holiday, we joined Pop in cutting and trimming trees for firewood and fence posts. Pop trained all of us in the use of a cross cut saw as soon as we were tall enough to keep from "riding" the saw. We had a tendency of dragging with some little weight when our sawing partner pulled the saw back. We learned to let the big crosscut glide with only its own weight to produce little effort for either party. We always were anxious for Pop to allow a brush pile to be burned while we were sawing. Not only did that mean warmth when Pop said to "take a blow", since we usually had several sweet potatoes in our coat pockets to be tucked in the coals and baked while we were cutting. Those hot, baked sweet potatoes were a real treat when we stopped to take a break. Pop seemed to delay the breaks, however, and when we asked to stop, he would say, "Just one more cut!", and then one more for at least several cut s.

***

The summer of 1935 was a duplicate of 1934, hot and dry. We would watch the dust clouds in the West and hear about the "Okies", the Kansas and Nebraska farmers leaving their farms for California and other Western areas. We always bought a Sunday newspaper, costing 10 cents and would see pictures of abandoned farms with dust and tumbleweeds piled high around their homes and fences. Our hill farm was not much better but we didn't have the strong winds and dust.

***

Bob and I came into possession of two tires which had been "rim cut" and discarded. A "rim cut" tire wouldn't stay on the rim and could not be repaired. We found a pastime in rolling the tires, similar to rolling a hoop. Ed Musterman had shown us how to turn the tire inside out, climb in and roll yourself down the hill. Since there was no method to steer the tire, this fun game produced bumps and bruises sufficient to convince us to abandon this sport in a short time! We were content to simply roll the tires ahead of us while Tom generally ran closely behind. One day we decided that "chipmunks" may make good pets and planned to catch one in our box rabbit traps. We set several traps near their burrows, just below the old barn, and would check them each evening after the days chores were finished. While checking the traps one evening, we were rolling the tires ahead with Bob in the lead and Tom following behind me. Bob was about 10 paces ahead of me and suddenly stopped, turned to me and I could see shock and panic in his eyes! "Ray, a snake just bit me!" he yelled! "Aw, you're kidding me, where did he bite you?" I was hoping he was wrong! "In the back!" he answered and then started to run! I looked at the ground and saw a fat copperhead. Bob had rolled his tire over the snake and then stepped on it. The snake had bitten Bob on the back of his foot! I turned to Tom and told him to run back the way we had come, that Bob had been bitten by a copperhead! I then ran after Bob, yelling, "Don't run, Bob, Pop said to never run if a snake bites you, don't run!" The more I shouted after him, the faster he ran! I couldn't keep up! We rounded the horse lot and started up the hill to the house. Mary was sitting on the cistern box and Bob was yelling to her, "Mary, a snake bit me!" When we reached the house, Mary had gotten Mom and she was there with a can of kerosene and some rags. She wrapped the rags around Bob's foot and then soaked them with kerosene. Ferd, Joe and Mom put Bob in the Model T truck and pushed it down the hill, hoping it would start! It did! Dr. DeFoe was the only doctor in the area and his office was in Hilltown, near where the Chesterfield Mall now stands. It was about four miles from our farm. Pop was really upset; he hated snakes and always feared that one of us would be bitten! We also always heard the horror tales of those who had been bitten, many of which were probably exaggerated. Pop told me to show him where the snake had been. I did, but the snake was no longer there! Pop wouldn't give up! He got a hoe and turned over every board near the pig pen, hot beds and around the old barn. At the rear of the barn was a wide oak board which was used as extra cover for the hot beds, when necessary. When Pop turned this board over, we saw a fat copperhead, all coiled. I don't know if this was the snake which bit Bob, but Pop called it a "sons a bitch" and killed it at least three times. Mom and the boys returned with Bob. The Doctor had run a probe into the bite and extracted what venom he could. Fortunately, only one of the snake's fangs penetrated Bob's ankle, while the other fang glanced off his shoe! His foot and leg were swollen to several times their normal size and Bob was in great pain. Bob and I shared the same bed in the shed addition to our house. He had trouble sleeping, due to the pain, and moaned and tossed well into the night. I had finally fallen asleep when Bob suddenly screamed and sat upright in bed! "Another snake just bit me!" he yelled, "Its in the bed with us!" Well, it didn't take long for both of us to be out of that bed! Mom always kept a kerosene lamp burning low at night and left on the kitchen table. She ran in with the lamp when Bob screamed and when she threw the sheet back, we saw a large red wasp. It had stung Bob on his back! Bob later made a crutch out of a sassafras sapling and hobbled around for several months before he could fully use his leg and foot again. We were always careful where we stepped but were extra careful after Bob's misfortune! We learned that snakes have a particular odor, which resembles over ripe apples and damp musty earth. We could often detect the odor and discover a snake in the area. Bob, in particular, was an expert at snake sniffing after he recovered from the bite! I know many people don't believe this and other hill country facts, but it is true!

***

Our cousin, Harold (Mike) Maisak, often spent a good part of the summer with us and we always looked forward to his visits. Harold was always energetic, willing to work, and a great help. He would stay with us, hoeing corn, weeding strawberries, shocking hay, or what ever the current job required. We had no hay rake and envied those neighbors who had a dump rake. Our hay was hand raked into "windrows", then shocked and hauled to the barn or stacked. We used long handled pitch forks to rake and shock the hay. The neighbors with dump rakes would use the horse drawn rake to put the hay into winrows, it would then be shocked by hand. This was a much speedier process than our method, but we had no other way of doing it. Harold liked to use the team to cultivate or plow and became quite good with them. They learned to understand his commands and we all got along very well.

The summer continued dry and scorching hot and work in the sun was draining. Harold still laughs when he recalls a the day when he and Bob were working the team in the field on a blistering hot day, both wishing to be out of the sun and under a shade tree. Pop came walking toward them in the field and yelled for them to stop! "Unhitch that team and get out of the field", Pop ordered. "You ought to know better than to work those animals in this heat!" He never mentioned Harold or Bob in the heat! Harold always chuckles when we talk of the incident.

Joe, Ferd and Boo would occasionally get a short term job with neighbors at hay or wheat harvest time. Joe had earned $2.00 by putting up hay during the summer for one of the neighbors. He probably should have stashed it in some safe place at the house, but he wanted to keep it with him, a decision which he would later regret! We had rented a field from the Haeussler's between our place and Kehrs Mill Road, and planted field corn on the parcel. Joe spent a day shucking corn at that field and when he returned home discovered that his $2.00 was missing! It must have worked out of his pocket! He was very upset! I went with him to look for the two one dollar bills and we retraced all of the steps Joe thought he had taken during the day. We never found the money! For several months we managed to go out of our way when in the general area to again look for the lost money but without success. Some field mouse probably lined his nest with Joe's two dollar bills.

Winter began early and proved to set a record for cold which stands to this day! Early in the winter, another cousin, Bill Abram, came out for a week end visit. He shared a bed with Joe in the shed addition to our house. Joe's bed was in the section with the bullet riddled piece of tin in place of a pane of glass for the window. In the morning, since the room was mighty cold and pretty dark, we always dressed by the wood range in the kitchen. Cousin Bill was a little modest, didn't want to go to the kitchen in his underwear, so decided to dress in the room. "How the heck do you see to get dressed in here, Joe?" Bill asked. "We just open the window!" Joe snapped and swung the window open on its hinges. As the icy wind whipped into the room, Bill forgot his modesty and decided that dressing with your rear to the kitchen range was a pretty good plan.

***

Although Christmas was never a time to expect great gifts, we anxiously looked forward to the holiday. Shortly before our school Christmas play, Uncle Bill Abram came out with gifts for each of us. He brought roller skates, some candy and a new pair of shoes for Mary! We had no place on the farm to roller skate, but we were thrilled with the gift. We would take the skates to school, in the spring, and skate home on the concrete pavement on Wild Horse Creek Road. We did just that and, while I'm sure it was rough on skates but they were well made and lasted a long time. On the night of the play Mary seemed to have trouble remembering her lines. She kept looking down at the floor and we wondered why she hesitated, since Mary was always mighty sharp in school! Mary later admitted that she had to keep admiring those beautiful new shoes and would be distracted while she missed her cue.

Mom and Pop always did the best they could to provide some gift for each of us at Christmas and we always appreciated what ever we got. We enjoyed looking through the Sears and Roebuck catalogue and wishing for some of the exciting things shown there. This winter, when we asked Mom what we would get for Christmas, she told us to look through the catalogue and select a toy as long as it didn't cost over 25 cents. We were excited! I selected a little metal car which cost 19 cents, and was described as being cast metal with genuine rubber tires. It sure sounded like a great gift and I was anxious for Christmas. The order was placed and the package arrived. A package from Sears was always an exciting event and we usually waited at our mailbox, at the end of our lane, for its arrival since it was usually too large to fit in the box. We delivered the unopened package to Mom, and knew that we would not see the contents until Christmas. On Christmas morning our selections were there and I had a beautiful little car about 3 inches long and it had genuine rubber tires! Several days after Christmas, we were visited by some classmates from school. They were the Backues boys, Clyde, Richard and Roy. Clyde was the eldest and Roy the youngest. Richard was my favorite and always seemed a cut above the others. When they asked what we got for Christmas, I ran and got my little car. Clyde asked to see it first and I handed it to him, while commenting on the genuine rubber tires. He appeared to be examining it closely, when suddenly he jerked the little tires off and threw them far into the woods! Well, I snapped! I got the nearest killing tool I could find, a corn knife, and attacked the three of them. The color drained from their faces and they ran in panic! I chased them as far as Andy Griffith's cabin, where I gave up the chase. Had I caught Clyde, I probably would have killed him. I warned them, that if they ever came on our place again, they would never leave! They never came back again!

***

That winter Pop got a job with the W P A ,building stone rip raps on the river bank down by the St. Louis County water works. He rode with Cliff Steiner, who also got a job there. The work was hard and dangerous in the icy cold but Pop was pleased to get it, though it would be only temporary.

Joe, Ferd and a friend, Harvey Koester, got a job from a St.Louis land owner to cut cord wood on his property in St. Louis County. They agreed to cut, split and stack 100 cords of wood on his property for $1.50 a cord. They each would receive 50 cents a cord and they were excited about the work. They worked all winter and completed the number of cords which were ordered. The caretaker of the estate complained that the cords were stacked wrong and that there was not a full cord in each stack! A cord is a stack 4 feet high, 4 feet wide and 8 feet long. The pieces were cut in two foot lengths as ordered. Pop went over to check the cords and to show the boys how to stack the wood. When the cords were stacked over, they had more cords than were ordered. Ferd was elected to collect their pay. Since the owner was only at his farm on weekends, Ferd went to see him on a Sunday, told him that 100 cords had been cut, delivered and stacked as ordered and the cords had been verified by his caretaker. Ferd then asked for their money which totaled $150.00. The land owner sat back and asked Ferd if he was familiar with the "Dunning Law!" Ferd was not! He then told

Ferd that the "Dunning Law" states that anyone who asks for payment of a debt or obligation on Sunday, violates the "Sunday Blue Law" provision in the Missouri statutes and therefore, no payment shall be made and the obligation is considered to be "Paid In Full!" Ferd was devastated! He came back to Joe and Harvey, who were waiting for him at the Haeussler farm, and told them the incredibly bad news!

Mrs. Haeussler came over to them and, sensing some serious problem, asked what had happened. Ferd told her the entire story. Mrs. Haeussler told Ferd to get in her car and she drove to the land owner's estate. A very short, heated directive from Mrs. Haeussler produced the money due to Ferd, Joe and Harvey. Ferd said that he didn't know what Mrs. Haeussler said but the land owner quickly backed away from his nasty bluff. The man was not successful in his attempt to cheat three country boys out of their winters work, a total of $150.00! Thanks again to Mrs. Haeussler!

Most of our neighbors were good, honest and helpful folks but, unfortunately, several who were not living near us proved to be less than honest and would be long remembered! A farmer needed some help cleaning his barn, the cattle lot and some corn shucking. Ferd went at an agreed price but discovered that one person could not complete the jobs requested in the time allotted. The farmer then agreed to hire Joe, also. The long tiring job was completed, only to learn that the farmer refused to pay them! Ferd wanted to burn down his barn, and he probably would if Pop not intervened! Pop eventually collected $7.00 from the farmer which was but a fraction of the original agreed payment! He told Pop that he just didn't have the money! Needless to say, our opinion of that man was less than respectable, but life went on just the same!

***

The weather continued bitter cold and our supply of staples were getting very low! The frost was inches thick on the kitchen windows and often the water bucket would freeze nearly solid during the night. Mom had old quilts, blankets and our coats piled on each bed, so that it was nearly impossible to turn over once you scooted under the covers. We would not have wanted to, anyway, since that would mean losing our warm spot. We left a small opening for breathing, and any exposure, other than our nose was not made! Pop always feared a flue fire and had a policy that no fire remained in the stove during the night and no wood fed to the range after 7:00 P M.

One day, Herb Weinrich came over and told us that one .of their cows had died. Pop asked what they were going to do with the dead cow and hide and Herb said they would bury it in the spring when the ground thawed. Pop asked if he could have the cow hide. He took the team to Weinrichs, found and skinned the dead cow. The hide and carcass was frozen hard, so he used the team to pull the hide from the carcass. The team shied from the dead animal, but Pop completed the job. After fleshing the hide later, he took it to a man in Chesterfield, who operated a truck freight service to St. Louis. He agreed to take the hide to the city where he got $1.00 for it. Pop bought $1.00 worth of flour from Andy Kroger's store and we stayed in biscuits and bread until the next source of income opportunity arose!

It was the policy of our school teachers, to give tests in each subject, prior to exams, to determine if a student could be excused from taking an exam in that particular course. The policy was an excellent one, in that most students studied harder for the tests than they would have for the exam. Miss Cuno's tests often consisted of as many as 500 questions. If our test grade was at least 80% and our class grades at least 80%, we would be excused from taking the exam and would be dismissed for the particular time allotted to that exam. I was excused from taking all, but one, of the exams in January 1936. The exam which I had to take was scheduled as the first one of the day, so I completed my papers, was excused, and started home alone. By the time I reached our lane, I was nearly frozen since the wind was directly out of the North and, we learned later, actual temperatures were at 16 below zero! They didn't measure wind chill, at that time, but it must have been 50 below zero. I decided to go down the embankment of the creek and follow the creek for a short distance, to be protected from the frigid wind. The creek was frozen over. I went through the ice at a spring and submerged to just above my waist, before being able to scoot out to the bank! My clothes froze as soon as the wind hit me and I scrambled up the bank and ran towards home! I had on a pair of Sears and Roebuck's "good" $1.98 boots, which were now soaked through and through! As I ran, I knew that I would have frost bite if I didn't get to the house quickly! My feet began to feel numb and, before I reached the house, it seemed as if I were running on wooden legs! My feet had no feeling other than a strange stiffness with each step! I quickly told Mom what had happened, she sat me on a chair in front of the range, opened the oven door, and pulled her chair up to face me. As she loosened my boot strings, little layers of ice fell to the floor! She held my feet between her hands on her warm lap until some feeling returned. She then fixed a pan of lukewarm water and held my feet in the pan. The water seemed very hot and soon my feet felt close to normal. I managed to escape with only minor frostbite of my feet and hands. The vivid memory of the cold winter of 1936 will always remain!

***

Early in the spring of 1936, Ferd agreed to help John Hager with some chores, with "pay" often being the exchange of work between close neighbors. Mom often planned a special treat when the older boys worked out, and would be tired and hungry when they returned home. That particular day, Mom prepared salmon croquettes. This was a real treat for us since salmon was about 10 cents a can! The dinner looked and smelled great as we all sat down to eat. I say, we all sat down, which really isn't correct, since Bob always stood at the dinner table. He said he could eat better that way, but there really weren't enough chairs for all of us anyway! We had just begun when Ferd threw down the salmon croquette he was eating, jumped up from the table, and ran outside! He was sick and throwing up! Everything stopped at the table! Pop had gone to attend to Ferd and returned shortly to tell us that Ferd said the salmon tasted funny and he was very sick! Pop sort of scolded Mom for having prepared that "damned fancy food!" Mom threw the salmon out and our hearts were heavy as she said, "Well, we'll just eat jelly bread!" Midge, our little dog, ate all of the salmon croquettes and we were quite envious of him! He didn't get sick either! It was some time before we learned the truth! John Hager had told Ferd that he had to smoke his corn cob pipe to prove he was a man, and he gave Ferd his pipe to try. The result was Ferd's first encounter with a strong pipe, strong tobacco and inhaling, all of which left him quite ill, and resulted in our loss of the salmon. We were unhappy with Ferd for some time, but eventually forgave him.

Later that spring, Ferd went to work for the Haeusslers and Joe went to work for Donald Barnes on Kehrs Mill Road. Joe and Ferd's pay were the same at $60.00 per month for 9 hours per day, six days a week. Joe occasionally had to go over to the Barnes farm on Sunday, also, to feed stock. They each gave Mom $30.00 per month for board and to help out. While their pay averaged only 20 cents or 25 cents per hour, they were pleased with the chance for a job and worked hard at it! Those jobs would continue until 1939.

The future started to look brighter with some members of the household bringing home pay, at the same time appetites were increasing, especially for Joe. He would often come home from work, snatch a freshly baked loaf of bread, and be two steps ahead of Mom, with her fly swatter! Joe would sometimes scurry into Mom's room, with the bread in his hand, throw himself on his back on the bed, and kick his feet wildly to fend off the swishing fly swatter! He would, also, often grab a full loaf of bread, break it in half, and eat it before supper. Joe, also, would on occasion, sneak into the root cellar, get a quart of Mom's peaches and consume it before supper. I always thought that Joe would be the largest in the family, but he wasn't, since Boo towered over the rest of us. I sat next to Joe at the table, and he ate so fast that he wouldn't slow down to ask for another slice of bread. He simply took mine off my plate! Joe sure could eat, but we all did rather well when it came to food!

Pop later went to work for the Haeusslers building a beautiful log cabin addition to the existing, small log cabin on their property. Boo worked for them also when they built a new barn on their property near Kehrs Mill Road. I believe that Haeussler's grandfather originally owned all of this property, which he sold to a man named Schneider, under a contract for deed. Schneider built the original small cabin. When he defaulted on his contract the Haeusslers had to take the farm back. The completed cabin addition was most impressive, with a huge stone fireplace in the main room. The Haeussler's farm was a real show place. Little did we then realize that, many years later, Chesterfield would become the prestige area of St.

Louis County, with many hundreds of homes even better than the beautiful log home on the ridge above Wild Horse Creek!

***

Ferd and Joe needed transportation to get to and from work and for all the other matters they felt young men should pursue. They found a 1929 Model A Sedan which they purchased for $125.00. They made a small down payment and financed the balance which called for payments of $7.00 per month. Pop was not very happy about the finance charge, and more than once, strongly commented that "Those damned cars were the ruination of the country!" I sometimes wonder if Pop wasn't close to being correct! This Model A opened a new world for us, however, and we managed to get to Overland to visit relatives, take in a movie at Valley Park and go to church in style! On one visit to Aunt Lou and Uncle George's house in Overland, we were given some apples for a snack before dinner. Bob, Tom and I were particularly impressed with the bathroom at their house and made a number of visits there. Bob was showing me how the toilet flushed, and he threw his apple core into the toilet! The bowl filled and started to overflow and we ran to tell Aunt Lou! She reached her arm down into the toilet bowl and retrieved the apple core. She wasn't too pleased with us as she said, "Don't you ever throw anything down the toilet!" We had been chastised and went out in the back yard to sulk! "We should never have thrown that apple in there, Bob", I said, trying to ease over the scolding. Bob just hung his head and said, "Well, hell! I always throw my apple cores in the toilet at home! "Of course "home" had an outhouse! We never threw anything else in toilet bowls, after that!

***

In late spring, Miss Cuno and Miss Jessie announced that a new park was to be dedicated in our area, and the unveiling ceremony would be conducted by our own Governor. She said this would be an historic event and we would all attend. The park, to be dedicated, was donated by Dr. Edmund Babler, and his statue was erected about 7 miles from the school. The teachers said that this was no problem, and that we would walk to the site, leaving at 9:00 A.M.for the ceremony at 2:00 P M. This turned out to be a long walk for many of the children and rides home in neighbor's cattle trucks were arranged. It turned out that the Governor couldn't make it and sent one of his subordinates, instead. We were disappointed that we didn't get to see the Governor and besides, we didn't understand much of what the official said at the dedication. The cleared site, for the statue, was located in a heavily wooded area and, to us, the park was not impressive. The Babler State Park is now a beautiful park and well used by St. Louis County residents.

***

The summer of 1936 was a repeat of the previous two summers with record breaking heat and no rain! We could often see rain squalls coming from the West, but they always seemed to change course as they reached the river and follow the stream. The "dust bowl" of the mid west continued and, at times, it seemed that our country would simply dry up and blow away! In spite of the heat and drought, crops were planted, including a field of pole beans, at the base of our hill. In late June or early July, huge swarms of large yellow grasshoppers (called locusts) converged on nearly everything that was growing! Pop said we should kill them by spraying with Arsenic of Lead, our only insecticide. I sprayed the beans several times, but without results, and decided that a stronger mix would do it. I tripled the amount of arsenic of lead per gallon of water and sprayed the bean crops heavily. Several days later, I checked the crop to find that all the beans were dead, but the grasshoppers were eating the dead leaves and chewing on the bean poles!

Bob and I were hoeing, one day near the house, and left our hoes in the field when Mom called us for lunch. When we returned, the grasshoppers had eaten a large part of our hoe handles where we gripped them, leaving a permeation of sweat! Those grasshoppers were hungry and mean little rascals! One day Mom sent Bob and me to investigate the bawling of our cows. We found them in a sassafras grove at the bottom of a draw near the Haeussler's line. The cows often went into that grove to be in the shade and to brush against the young saplings to chase the flies. The cows were swinging their necks, stamping and bawling pitifully! We were startled to see grasshoppers in groups of three or four, on their backs where the cows had been bitten by horseflies! The grasshoppers had eaten into their flesh to a depth of about 1/2 or 3/4 inch! We knocked the grasshoppers off, took the cows to the barn and Mom had us put wagon axle grease over the wounds. We applied wagon axle grease to each horsefly bite daily, after that, until the grasshopper attack was ended!

***

Fall was welcome, with cooler weather, and the early winter opened the trapping season. We had a number of box rabbit traps and could sell a dressed wild rabbit for 15cents and often 25 cents to Miss Jessie or to some folks in town. In addition, Bob had a number of steel traps set along the creek and a few in the woods near or in persimmon groves. The bulk of his catch was Muskrat which, when skinned, stretched and partially cured, could be shipped to Chicago where they would bring as little as 75 cents for a "kit" (young muskrat) to as much as $3.00 for a large pelt. An occasional opossum or raccoon would be caught and, they also would fetch a payment. I often accompanied Bob on his 5:00 AM trips and marveled at how skilled he was with the sets! The money from the sale of his pelts bought boots, overalls and shirts. One day, as we were returning from the "run" we neared the last set, which was in a persimmon grove, about 100 yards east of the house. One trap held a large skunk who was not very pleased with his misfortune. Bob and I agreed that the prudent thing to do was to go to the house for the 22 rifle, shoot him and then remove him from the trap. We rarely shot trapped animals since any hole in the pelt would reduce the value considerably. When Pop saw us with the rifle, he wanted to know what we were going to do. We told him. "No, don't do that, you'll ruin the pelt!" Pop scolded. We told Pop that we would shoot him through the head and that wouldn't depreciate the pelt very much. "That's the trouble with you kids", Pop said, "You want to do it the easy way and risk spoiling the hide, let me get a long pole and I'll show how to take care of the skunk and not damage the hide!" Pop picked the longest clothes prop we had and followed us to the grove. He approached the skunk, within striking distance, and raised the pole. As he struck, the skunk seemed to back up, arch his back and tail, and a fine powerful mist covered the area, including Pop! The skunk was quite conscious as Pop repeated the process with the clothes pole and, as he struck, the skunk repeated his artful spraying process! This time the odor was much more powerful and had greater range. Pop threw the clothes pole on the ground, turned to Bob, and with eyes blazing, shouted, "Shoot that sons-a-bitch!" The skunk made a very pretty pelt but, for some reason, was rejected by the fur buyer. Probably too many bruises on the hide!

***

The spring of 1937 seemed to be a turning point in the severe weather patterns which were crippling the nation. Warm rains and mild weather allowed normal plantings and our outlook improved. The crops seemed to be doing well and we managed to keep the weeds down with those "sharp hoes" which were always provided by Pop.

Our next "hill" neighbors, the Hawkins, were now required, by law, to attend school at the little one room school house, for blacks, on the banks of the creek, and we would meet them often on our way home on the lane. They always stopped at the spring, at the end of our lane, to fill their gallon Karo syrup pails with water. They had no cistern or permanent water source at their shack. Several .of the children were probably in their teens when they first attended school and were learning to read the first grade primer. We always asked what they learned that day, and Nellie, one of the girls, was quite proud to demonstrate her reading ability. She would open her primer and read, or pretend to read, "Ah see a dog!" Then she would giggle and hang her head as though she were embarrassed. We would then praise her efforts which usually prompted a second reading, "Ah see a cat!" Further praise seemed to embarrass her and she would reach out and strip a poison ivy vine growing along the lane! We watched with awe and concern as she then would put the poison ivy in her mouth and eat it! Somehow, she never seemed to get poison ivy. Primitive conditions were now meeting some formal education efforts on the hills around Wild Horse Creek!

Tony Reuther planted a field of corn along our lane at the

bottom of our field. It was on property which he owned, a long narrow strip running parallel to our lane, and adjoining an old apple orchard at the base of our hill. We had a short cut from town or school, which took us across this field and over a path through this orchard. This was the same orchard where Pop said the "Little Old Woman" would jump on your back from the trees, so we only used this path during the day! One day, Bob and I were taking this short cut and as we reached the orchard, we heard voices! We stopped and listened. It was two of the Hawkin boys, coming along the lane next to the corn field. They were speaking in their own language and we decided to hide in the orchard, to see if we could understand anything they were saying. They stopped about 50 yards from where we were hiding and entered the corn field. We kept hidden and watched. They unfolded several sacks and jabbered excitedly. We looked at each other and said, "It looks like they are going to take some of Mr. Reuther's corn, let's go warn them how wrong that would be!" They were shocked as we emerged from our hiding and approached them! We told them that they shouldn't take any of that man's corn and if they asked him, he may give them some. They stood there, holding their sacks and adamantly denied that they were planning to take any corn! We left, after warning them that they should never do that! They were not happy! That evening, George Hawkins, their father, came up the hill and met us near the house, where he asked to see Pop. Mr. Hawkins always carried a walking stick and seemed to have a problem with one eye which was always nearly half closed. This may be the reason that he cocked his head to one side as he was listening or wanted to make a point. When doing that, the good eye seemed to be much larger, and the half closed eye would rise slightly! We got Pop and stood by to see what Mr. Hawkins wanted. He started, "Mr.

Ruby, yo boys done 'cused my boys of stealin, now my boys don't steal an I don't like that! Now, iff'n yo boys evah 'cuse my boys of stealin sumpin just might happen to yo boys! yo unnastan?" Then he cocked his head to await Pop's reply. Pop treated everyone with the greatest respect, regardless of status or color and considered this family to be good neighbors, but it was not wise to threaten his family! From the corner of my eye, I could see fire flash in Pop's eyes, as he said, "What did you say? Repeat that again!" Mr. Hawkins slowly started over, "Ah said, if yo boys 'cuse my boys of stealin, sumpin might happen to yo boys, yo unnastan?" Pop snapped his reply, as he moved closer to Mr. Hawkins. Now if you or your family ever harm my boys, there will be dead Hawkins lying all over these hills! You understand!" Mr. Hawkins stepped back several feet and I watched the bad eye jerk and his head twitch as he said, "Yassuh, I unastan, I don think anythin will evah happen to yo boys!" With that, Mr. Hawkins left and the incident was closed.. A strained relationship existed afterward, however, and an incident with the youngest boy occurred the following year. I'll describe that incident later.

***

School attendance represented a great part of our social life and, while we complained about homework and the teachers, we were actually quite fond of both Miss Jessie and Miss Cuno. I have always felt indebted to these two women for the quality of their teaching ability, their general example and their dedication. I regret that I had not made the effort to look them up, in later years, to let them know how much their efforts influenced my life!

***

While Mom now had some limited income from the boys outside employment and from what we could produce on the farm, the years were lean and we knew that she had a very difficult time in making ends meet! The Christmas of 1937 was eagerly anticipated and we always wondered what we would get! A package had arrived from Sears Roebuck and Mom's order was carefully tucked away on the shelf of her closet. Mom walked to church, for choir practice, one night the week before Christmas, and while she was gone, we hinted to Pop that he might give us some clue as to our gift. He finally decided to show us. Each of the younger boys was to get a pair of bib overalls. I don't remember what Mary was to get. Pop made us promise not to tell Mom that he had shown us our gift. We promised, as we tried to hide our disappointment! We knew that these were lean times and we loved Mom and Pop for the sacrifices and effort which they made for all of us.

I was becoming more observant of some of the little things which affect the lives of a large family in poor times. One thing I always noticed, and I don't know if the others noticed it, but Pop was never very hungry if the meal looked as though it would barely go around. He always made certain that everyone had enough meat, before he took a small piece! He also seemed to be especially fond of the fat on pork and bacon, which most of us would rather pass. His concern for the family was something that I'll always remember!

***

Aunt Ella and Uncle Joe VanClooster, Pop's sister and brother in law, held the mortgage on our farm, with a balance of $1,000.00 and interest payable once each year. In the fall of 1937, Mom wrote to them shortly before the interest was due, and asked if we could pay the interest in the spring, when the strawberry crop came in. Uncle Joe said that was OK. They drove out frequently on Sundays, when the weather was nice, and would visit for several hours. Pop always managed to send apples, sweet potatoes and the choice selections of what ever was in season, so that they returned home with some of our best produce. Shortly after Christmas, they came for a Sunday visit and Mom asked Aunt Ella if they had a nice Christmas. She said, "Well, we couldn't do all the things we wanted to because SOME people couldn't pay the interest on their loan and we just had to sacrifice!" Mom was crushed! She and Pop then began diligently to find some way to refinance the mortgage so that Aunt Ella would not have to sacrifice anything again. That avenue was opened when Pop talked to Mrs. Haeussler regarding the loan and a refinancing was arranged. Pop agreed to convey a small corner of our property to the Haeusslers so that they would have access to their property off Wild Horse Creek Road, over our lane, entering their property at the base of our hill. He then borrowed $1500.00 from them on a mortgage to pay Aunt Ella her $1,000.00, buy a team of mules from the Stockyards in East St. Louis and provide some cash for farm working capital. We then owned Julie and Bell, the mule team, one of which would be with us for a long time. Julie was a gentle sweetheart but Bell was a terror. It seemed that Boo was the only one who could manage Bell without being bitten or kicked! The day after Julie and Bell arrived I had an encounter with Bell which left me feeling insecure around horses and mules for a long time. Bob and I had decided to try smoking, since that seemed to be what every older boy did. Pop only bought Bull Durham tobacco which came in a small cloth sack had two packs of cigarette papers attached and sold for 5 cents. Pop was mighty particular about his tobacco and would never be without it. He could roll his cigarettes with the skill of a cowboy! We wouldn't dare take any of Pop's tobacco, so we decide to retrieve cigarette butts and save the remains for a fresh roll. The best place to find butts which weren't too badly damaged was the wood floor of the outhouse. From that location, Bob and I collected them daily, peeled the butts and put the tobacco in a small glass jar, which we hid in a small playhouse located at the far end of the horse lot. I thought that Pop wouldn't miss one package of his cigarette papers, so I removed one package from his sack and hid them in the playhouse, along with the jar of tobacco. Several days later, a furor erupted at the house. It seemed that Pop was out of tobacco papers and Mom was searching diligently for some. As the furor increased, I decided that removing Pop's tobacco papers was not wise and, somehow, they should be replaced! I started for the playhouse and entered the horse lot. Bell looked at me, curled her lips and laid her ears back! I spoke softly to her as I extended my hand, as if to pet her. Her lip curled further and her ears tightened against her head! I still continued, since I thought it would be a lesser risk facing an irritable mule, than to face Pop without his cigarettes! When I was approximately half way across the lot, Bell charged me and as I turned to escape by the shortest way, I fell! Bell reared and struck at me with her front hooves, as I rolled over and over, trying to regain my footing! She raced past me and turned to charge again, as I finally got on my feet. I raced down the lot and broad jumped the five foot fence to safety! I really couldn't jump that high or move that fast, but that day I did! The plan to retrieve Pop's papers was abandoned and after a little more furor, Pop went to Chesterfield to purchase some more Bull Durham. I decided that smoking was hazardous to my health, a fact that was proven by the US Surgeon General many years later!

Bell wasn't with us very long and, when she died, Pop bought Bill, a fine young horse, for $50.00. Bill and Julie worked well together for a number of years and made a fine team. Bill was only about four years old when we got him, and lived long after Pop sold the farm.

***

Times were changing, and occasionally the truant officers from St. Louis County would come in our area to track down some of our black neighbors who refused to attend school. It seemed that some were much too old to attend, and refused, while others were most anxious to attend. Since schools were segregated, I have no idea what went on in the one room school for blacks, on the banks of the creek. One of the Hawkin boys, the youngest, named Homer, attended with some regularity and seemed to have developed an antagonistic attitude toward us, as we often met him on our way home from school. One day, as Tom and I were walking home, Homer (we called him O'Mar) was waiting for us by the spring, at the entrance to our lane. He joined us as we walked and when we reached the turn off lane to Andy Griffin's house, "O'Mar" turned to Tom and asked, "Tommy, whar do ah go to school?" Since we were just across the creek from the school, and it was still visible, Tom merely turned and pointed to the school house as he said, "Why O'Mar, you go to that school". O'Mar said, "No, Tommy, what do yo call that school?" Tom hesitated, then said, "Why, I call that YOUR school, that is where you go". O'Mar was getting more antagonistic as he asked again, "But what do yo call that school, Tommy?" I knew that he was baiting Tom, trying to draw him into a fight, and I could feel my blood moving up around my ears and throat! When Tom didn't answer, O'Mar pushed further, "Ah asked yo what yo called that school,

Tommy!" With that, I turned to O'Mar and said, "We call that the NIGGER SCHOOL, that is what you wanted Tom to say, isn't it?" It was! O'Mar just leaped back, and with fire in his eyes, shouted, "Don yo evah say that word agin, heah me! Ah'l tromp yo if yo evah say that word agin!" By this time, my temper had reached a reckless point! I charged right up to his face, told him that he was baiting Tom, wouldn't let up and was acting like you wanted to start a fight! O'Mar then ran into the ditch in front of Andy's house, threatening as he ran! He came out of the ditch with his hands filled with large rocks, saying he was going to rock us to death! I charged at him and he retreated! I dared him to throw just one rock! "Please throw the first rock, O'Mar, and I'll have an excuse for tearing your damned arms off, 'cause I'm going to tear you apart, piece by piece!" He kept retreating as I followed him to the base of Arbuckle's hill, hoping that he would throw a rock! He never did! We had no further trouble with O'Mar and he gave us a wide berth after that! Tom was impressed and decided that I was some sort of protector who would fight anyone who crossed either of us. This reasoning of Tom's caused me one heck of a bruise on the side of my head and a sore jaw, just weeks after the O'Mar incident!

We had a family named Penick, in our school, with the oldest boy about 12 or 13 years old and in the fourth grade. His name was William and considered himself the school bully! I had nothing to do with him but liked the rest of the family. It seemed that Tom chose to have some disagreement with William and told him that I could whip him anytime. William was furious and anxious to prove how good he was! I knew nothing of Tom's challenge when Tom asked me to wait for him at our mailbox, since he would be just a little late. Tom had told William that I would be waiting at the mailbox to take him down a notch or two! I stood at the mailbox and watched William approach. He looked strange and his pace quickened as he neared me. I wondered what he wanted! When he came up to me, he swung a hard right to the side of my head, knocked me down and, as I tried to get up, he hit me in the jaw with another right! I never even got my arms up! He then stalked away, shouting, "That'll teach you!" I couldn't put together what had happened! My head was still spinning when Tom came ambling down the road. Tom's first comment pretty well cleared the matter as he said, "I'll bet you sure took William down a notch, huh?" I had the urge to tromp Tom but I was still pretty groggy and decided to forgive him, after he promised never to do that again. I never explained anything to William and, while we were never friends, we did talk on occasion.

***

When the electric company ran their lines along Wild Horse Creek Road, a private telephone company had followed. This company was owned and managed by Walter Plein. Mr. and Mrs. Plein operated the switchboard above the bank and post office in the village of Chesterfield, across from Andy Kroger's old general store. The Pleins had one daughter named Doris. When Doris started in our school, I fell in love! Doris was a little on the "plump" side but she had pretty hair, a sweet voice and her skin looked very soft! It was the spring of 1938 when I really wanted Doris to know how *I* felt about her and had the opportunity when she asked me to write in her autograph book. I wrote something to the effect that she was the prettiest girl I knew, but I don't remember the exact words. It generated no response from Doris! Actually, there were not too many girls to choose from, in our school, and when it was narrowed down to Catholic girls, there was only Doris and Helen Honigfort, at that time. I thought that I had to find a Catholic girl, since Mom was not likely to approve of a Protestant, and I was thinking "long term!" Helen Honigfort was an intelligent girl, had freckles and was kind of cute. She had one habit, however, which caused me some difficulty. She chewed the eraser off her pencils!

I finally got an autograph book of my own and was anxious to find out how Doris really felt about me. I asked her to write in my book. She wrote: "Remember well, and keep in mind, that real true friends are hard to find, and when you find one just and true, exchange not the old ones for the new!" I tried to read something romantic into that, but it just wasn't there!

I later had to retire my beautiful green velvet covered autograph book, when only a few had written in it. I had asked Ferd to write in my book and, to my surprise, he agreed. He wrote the following on the back side of the page on which Doris had written: "WHEN YOU ARE PLAYING WITH A LITTLE TURD, THINK OF YOUR POOR OLD BROTHER, FERD!" Well, I couldn't tear out the page and couldn't have anyone else write in there, since all read what had been written, and I didn't want them to see Ferd's poetry. Since ink eradicator was not yet available I tried to erase the word "TURD"! No luck ! I then carefully altered it to look like "BIRD". It would now read, "When you are playing with a little bird, think of you poor old brother, Ferd". I knew that didn't make much sense and "bird" still looked like "turd" so I filed the book away in my dresser drawer. If I ever got another 25 cents I could buy a new one and start over. I never did!

I didn't give up on Doris. I washed carefully behind my ears, combed my hair neatly and always tried to look intelligent in her presence. One day in late spring before school was out, at noon lunch break, I went to the field which adjoined the school, and lay down in a thick stand of red clover. Doris came around the building and saw me! She ran gracefully toward me and my heart beat wildly! She came right up to me and sat in the clover beside me. I was speechless! She then said, "Raymond, may I ask you a very personal question?" "Absolutely"! I answered, "Anything you would like!" This was it, I thought. Then she asked, "Does Bob like me?" I thought, Oh damn! Those baby blue eyes of Bob's and that handsome innocent face did it to me! I tried to sound nonchalant when I answered, "Sure, Bob likes everybody!" I was still hoping that this Bob interest would not expand. "No, I mean does he really like ME?" I guess so, Doris, but I'll see what I can find out for you". She thanked me and ran back to the school. I knew that all the girls liked Bob and realized that I must scratch Doris from my list! That left only one Catholic girl, Helen! I thought about Helen for a while but soon abandoned that idea, since I didn't want to lose the eraser off my pencil! Maybe I would just have to consider a Protestant! There were several really cute Protestant girls in school but I don't think they even knew I existed! I doubt if Helen did either! Doris stopped coming to church on Sunday and I felt better about the failed relationship.

***

Cousin Harold spent part of the summer with us, as did Tudor and Shirley. Cousin Al, Harold's brother, had spent two weeks with us one previous summer, but he and Tom drowned some baby chicks while he was there, and the scolding they both received from Mom discouraged future extended visits! While Tudor and Shirley were visiting, I learned of an event

which would take place in Wild Horse Creek, which I thought
Tudor would like to witness. It was the Baptism ceremonies of
the black congregations from around the area. On the scheduled
day, I took Tudor through the woods to a bank overlooking
the creek, where we could watch! All of the participants were
clothed in white garments and the Pastor entered the stream
first. Each participant, in turn would approach him, profess
their faith in loud voice, and be dunked completely under. All
of the observers kept up a chant or continuous singing. I had
seen this all before, but Tudor was most impressed, and never
forgot the incident!

***

Pop and Mom, together with financial help from Ferd and
Joe, felt that they could now complete an addition to the house
to provide much needed room. Pop dug a basement on the East
side of the house, using our team and a slip, along with a lot
of hand effort. The existing structure had only a crawl space,
so that storage was limited. Wayne Kimler and Ed Musterman
came out after the foundation was in and helped Pop and the
older boys frame in the addition. It ran the length of the house
and would consist of one large room for a living and dining
area. A number of windows would be on the East side with
an outside entrance door on the Southwest side. A chimney
for a free standing stove was built by Pop on the North side,
with a small window on each side of the chimney. When Pop
got the brickwork for the chimney out of the ground, Uncle
Bill Abram sent one of his bricklayers out to complete the
job. It looked good! The room couldn't be completed in one
weekend so we had to wait for Wayne to return the following
weekend. Unfortunately, it rained and rained that week and,
since the windows had not been installed, the floor of 1x6 pine

had warped! There was nothing that could be done! If we had electricity, I suppose they could have been sanded, but since it was not available, the floors remained warped. Mom was disappointed with that but we lived with linoleum covering our "groovy" floors. When the room was completed, Mrs. Haeussler gave us a walnut dining room set and the room was complete! It was great! We knew that someday the shed addition on the West would also be replaced and then our entire house would be complete. That addition was finally made some years later.

***

I often ponder about the years while we were on the old hill farm and realize that the Good Lord must have been watching over that large, poor family! We escaped many illnesses and serious accidents, while occasions for accidents were plentiful. A visit from or to the doctor was really rare, and fortunately so since we had no means to pay him. The Doctor serving that area was Dr. DeFoe, and he lived in a two story house at the corner of Olive Street Road and Clarkson Road. We provided Dr. DeFoe with some tomato plants in the spring and some strawberries on occasion in the season. He always said that was pay enough! He was a very homely man with a good sense of humor and a very big heart. He liked to repeat Abraham Lincoln's favorite comment about appearance, which suggested that he was the ugliest man alive and if he ever saw one uglier, he would shoot him. Well, he said he did see an uglier man one day but didn't shoot him because he felt so sorry for that ugly son of a gun! Then the doctor would grin. Other than Mom's malaria and Bob's snake bite, we had few occasions to seek the doctor's help. He came to the farm once when both Bob and I were sick and Mom couldn't diagnose the illness from her old "Doctor's Book", which she stored on the shelf in her closet. Our remedies mostly consisted of castor oil, turpentine, cough syrup and Vicks salve. • When Dr. DeFoe examined Bob and me, he gave Mom a bottle of black looking liquid and told her that we just had lazy biles. Well, Mom didn't allow anything to be lazy very long around our house and she gave us the medicine. Our rectums burned for two days as the nasty tasting medicine stirred up and evacuated whatever was lazy about our "biles" and we both then felt fine.

My only trip to Dr. DeFoe's home was the result of a strange accident. I had gathered a wheelbarrow full of weeds to feed the hogs, and was running down the hill to the hog lot, pushing the wheelbarrow ahead of me. A bracket, in front of the wheel, came loose and one side gouged into the earth, flipping me over the wheelbarrow. My left pants leg was torn and I felt the warm blood running down my leg! I felt no pain, but as I tried to get up, I found that I couldn't stand on my left leg. The leg was numb and the blood was running into my shoe! I managed to hobble to the house, where Mom ripped the pants leg open, saw the gouged out section of my leg and then poured turpentine into the open wound! It didn't burn at first, but I knew that I had the turpentine treatment shortly afterward! When Joe and Ferd came home from work, Mom took me to Dr. DeFoe's. He was out on a call. As we waited for his return, a threatening storm was approaching and finally the decision was made to return home! No doctor visit and I was glad! Unfortunately, the leg would not heal although Mom bathed it daily with warm water, cleansing the wound and applying fresh bandages. She forbade me to swim in the creek with the rest of the family. After several weeks, I started going to the creek with the others, promising that I wouldn't go in the water. One day, while I watched the others swim in that cold, clear water, I decided to launch and ride our small log raft. I promptly slipped off one side, when the raft tipped, and my injured leg got all wet! Since I was already wet, I thought that I may as well go swimming. Mom would understand! After about an hour in the water, I looked at my leg and was surprised to see that the wound was washed clean, leaving the leg looking blue around the injury! It looked better than it had since the accident! I told Mom what had happened and what I did. She was pleasantly surprised when she saw how good my leg looked, and told me to go swimming in the creek every day. I did! Within a couple of weeks my leg was completely healed. I guess the cold water, or something in the water speeded the process!

Bob had another trip to the doctor's home, as a result of an accident which was play or recreation related. Just west of the house, on the hill, and across from the old barn, the hill dropped steeply into a V shaped valley. Huge oaks and hickory trees grew on both slopes. Large grape vines hung from several of the oaks and one was cut to make a grapevine swing. By holding onto the vine and swinging across the ravine, you could drop safely on the other side. Bob made a bad drop and cracked several ribs. Dr. DeFoe had him wrapped with wide tape to resemble a "mummy". It took some time to heal and we were glad it was not more serious. When Boo later dropped off the vine, into the draw, and landed in a yellow jackets nest, the vine came down! Pop had to rescue Bob and me from the bees. Pop, Bob and I had numerous bee stings but I don't remember Boo and Tom having any! The bees followed us to the house and circled the house for a while! They were pretty angry!

The most serious accident involved Ferd while he worked at the Haeusslers. They had purchased a Palomino mare and her colt, neither of which had been broken to harness. The mare had been broken to saddle, but the colt had not. Ferd was always good with horses, so he and Harry Haeussler broke the colt to saddle and started the harness breaking. Shortly before the breaking process was completed, they had the horses shod. Harry and Ferd hitched the mare to a sulky to test the breaking results. The mare started off 0 K but then became frightened, went a little crazy and started kicking over the traces, breaking away from the sulky! When Ferd tried to restrain her, she reared and struck at him with her front legs. One shoe caught Ferd along the side of his head and peeled his ear back along his head! The horse ran on! Harry picked Ferd up and they rushed him to the hospital! Ferd never lost consciousness and endured the many stitches without benefit of painkillers. The doctor said that they could not use anything due to the location of the injury! Fortunately, Ferd fully recovered and the injury only delayed his entry into the military service by a few months. Harry Haeussler was also the victim of a serious farm injury from which he miraculously fully recovered! When I later sold and delivered some red raspberries to Mrs. Haeussler, I had to walk through the pasture where the horses grazed. Due to Ferd's accident and my previous experience with these four legged creatures, I gave them a wide berth!

***

The long drought seemed to have ended, and reasonable rainfall improved crops, pasture and spirits. Income realized from Joe, Ferd, Boo and Pop, while modest, contributed greatly to our improved lifestyle. Bob, also got a few days work on occasion. A farmer came over one day to see if he could get some help with the plowing, since he and his family wanted to go to the Missouri State Fair. Bob was the only one available, but said that he could do it. He took the job and completed it in record time. The farmer was impressed, but he paid Bob 1/2 the amount he said he would have had to pay a "nigger" while commenting that Bob did more work in one day than most grown men do in two. Bob collected his $2.00 but we all felt that he had not been treated fairly.

***

A small movie theatre opened in Manchester, Mo. on Manchester Road and they had several programs to entice patrons to spend 25cent for adults and 10cents for children's admissions. Cups, saucers and plates were sometimes given to the adults. The theatre then sponsored an amateur night with prizes of $3.00 for first place winner, $2.00 for second and $1.00 for third. Mom agreed that I could enter as a stand up minstrel. Contestants were allowed free admission, so I figured that I couldn't lose. I'd be 10cents ahead, get to see the movie and have a chance at one of the prizes. I appeared with an "Afro" wig, checkered coat and large bow tie, all of which was made by Mom. My face was blackened and I presented my one man performance. I won second place and collected $2.00! We were delighted!

Mrs. Haeussler gave Ferd and Joe a beautiful Crosley, battery powered radio for their 21st birthday. The radio required both large and small batteries for operation and listening times were rationed. This was long before transistors were invented and standard batteries had a relatively short life. This radio was the greatest gift that Mrs. Haeussler could have given and it provided us with a great amount of enjoyment.

Brother-in-law Wayne got Boo a job with Brunson Construction, as a carpenter apprentice, in early 1939 and Boo went to Columbia, Missouri to work. He later went to Cape Girardeau to work on the State University being constructed there. Joe and Ferd also went into construction in 1939, as carpenter apprentices, and their income situation also greatly improved. Construction wages paid to Boo, Ferd and Joe were 87½ cents per hour for $7.00 per day and $35.00 per week. At that time, gasoline was 12½ cents per gallon, bread 10 cents a loaf and a new auto cost about $600.00! While construction wages were low, they beat farm labor wages and everyone felt indebted to Wayne for his help in getting these jobs.

Joe bought a 1932 Ford V/8, which was the first V/8 that Ford made. It was fast and had more pick-up than Joe and Ferd were used to, so Joe placed a 2x4 beneath the accelerator to prevent anyone from having a "heavy foot". Ferd bought a Chevrolet coupe and started dating. Times were changing on the old hill farm!

The radio, along with the Sunday newspaper brought us the news of the country and the world. The Sunday newspaper at 10 cents would normally have been considered a luxury, which we could do without, but was always justified due to the many uses it served. It was read page by page by Mom and Pop provided the wrapping for lunches, became the fire starter for kindling in the wood cook stove in the morning,, covered the chamber pot on cold winter nights and finally, provided wiping material in the outhouse. No part of the paper was wasted. Few purchases in the 20th century provided as much mileage as that 10 cent Sunday paper.

***

Pop had been concerned at what was happening in Europe and Africa, since Italian Dictator Benito Mussolini had his troops invade Ethiopia in 1935. At that time, he hoped for the Ethiopians to somehow win. Haile Selassie's Ethiopian warriors were armed with only spears, sticks and ancient weapons, while the Mussolini forces had tanks and modern war weapons, and yet, Pop seemed to think they could win! He always pulled for the "little guys" and would wish those "Epiopians" (as Pop called them) would wipe out those "sonsabitches". Of course, that never happened and, when Adolph Hitler sent his troops into the Rhineland in 1936, Pop added another "sonsabitch" to the group. Hitler was considered a "good man" by many German residents of the U.S.A. and, even after he invaded Austria in 1938 and started World War 2 by invading Poland in 1939, he continued to be regarded as good for the German people! Comments from some area folks about Hitler being a "good man" alienated Pop's relationship with some. These comments by some members of Ascension Church and remarks about Pop doing some work for the Catholic Church as "butting in" brought Pop and others to a near combative situation. Pop wanted to "stomp some heads in" but Mom soothed the situation and was careful to keep Pop away from town. Pop had a better perception of the world situation than many well educated and informed individuals! He feared war as a result of what was happening with the Axis powers but our country continued to be rather complacent! Europe was a long way from us and our country was still struggling back from a most serious depression.

With Joe, Ferd, Boo and Pop working, the farm chores fell to Bob, Tom and to me. I got one of the wildest rides of my life unexpectedly one day, when Bob and I were plowing a small parcel of ground which we had rented from a neighbor. This parcel was at a bend in the creek and was generally cooler in that area due to the current and flow of the water around the bend. That area was previously named "the ice box" by Boo, and we would often arrange to stop there, beneath a huge mulberry tree, to eat our lunch. When we worked a distance from the house, Mom would send Mary with our lunch. She usually sent hot coffee in a gallon Karo syrup bucket, and wrapped our jelly sandwiches in some newspapers. We shared a cup which Mary also brought. We usually brought our drinking water with us when we started out in the morning. We carried the water in a gallon crockery jug wrapped with a burlap sack. By dipping the sack and jug into the creek occasionally, the water would remain fresh and cool through evaporation. Mary would sometimes stay and talk with us, until we finished our lunch, but, on this particular day she could not stay, since Mom needed her at the house for something and besides, the sky looked like rain! When we finished eating, Bob put the cup inside the Karo can and we left it beneath the mulberry tree. We made a few rounds of furrows, after lunch, and noticed that the sky was becoming dark and threatening! Since we were in a valley, the storm was nearly upon us before we saw how serious it appeared! Bob ordered the team to be unhitched and he would ride Bill and I ride Julie. At the last minute I remembered the coffee bucket and picked it up and hung the bail over one of Julie's hames. The team had all their harness on and their traces were hooked into the harness. We swung up on their backs as Bob said, "Let's race to the barn and beat this storm!" With Bob on Bill, a very fast horse, and me on Julie, a faithful mule, I realized that the race would be "no contest" and expected Bob to win by a quarter of a mile! When the coffee cup started to rattle inside the Karo syrup can, Julie's ears turned 180 degrees and she took off on the fastest legs I ever dreamed possible! The harness straps were snapping at some very private and tender parts of my anatomy as I sawed on Julie's bridle and pleaded with her to slow down! She wouldn't listen! I tried to remove the bucket from her hames, but I was bouncing so hard and holding on so tight, this effort was not successful! I passed Bob and Bill after only about 100 yards and reached the barn much ahead of them. Unfortunately, Julie didn't stop at the gate or the barn door, but I stopped rather abruptly at the barn door! Although I won the race and we beat the heavy storm, I was not pleased with the results! I was concerned, for a time, if I would ever be able to father any children! As it turned out, that concern and worry was not necessary!

Some other chores were new to us and seemed to be laced with risk but also some excitement. One day as Tom and I carried water and a scoop of bran to "Bessie", our cow, she reared up and tried to place her feet on Tom's shoulders. Tom didn't stay there very long! I knew that this was a sign that "Bessie" was in heat, but I wasn't about to say anything to Mom! Tom had no inhibitions, however, and not knowing what Bessie was signaling, ran to Mom yelling, "Mom, Bessie tried to ride me, she wanted to jump on my back!" I was embarrassed! Later that day, Mom called Bob and me and told us to take the cow to Dr. Arbuckle's farm to be bred to their Hereford bull. The next morning, Bob and I led Bessie to the encounter or rather, Bessie led us! I was rather apprehensive about this encounter but Bob said "No problem!" When we entered the pasture, just above where Boo built his house, the Hereford bull bellowed from up on the hill near where the Harman's house stood. Bessie started running uphill and the bull came roaring downhill! He looked larger than an elephant to me and I strongly suggested (pleaded) with Bob that we leave Bessie and get the hell out of there! Bob appeared calm and said we must stay with the cow to make sure she'd be all right! I wondered what "not being all right" would be and what we would do about it if she were "not all right!" I didn't want to take time to ask! When the bull was about 100 feet away, I decided that Bessie would have to deal with the encounter without my moral assistance and *I* retreated to a grove of sassafras trees nearby. Bob stayed and held onto Bessie's lead rope as she seemed to welcome a more vigorous than amorous meeting.

After what seemed an awfully long time, we led Bessie back home, as I watched over my shoulders to make sure the bull would not mistake either Bob or me for another cow! Several days passed and Bessie repeated her attempted ride, on my shoulders this time. Tom wouldn't go near her! Mom called Bob and me again and said that we should now take Bessie to be bred by Tony Reuther's Black Angus bull, since apparently the Hereford breeding didn't "take!" That seemed odd to me since Bessie sure "took" and the bull sure "gave", but Mom sure knew a lot more about these cows than we did! The next morning, Bessie led Bob and me along the lane at a fast trot. By the time we reached Wild Horse Creek Road, the trot was a full blown gallop! Bessie seemed to know where she was going! We entered the pasture, just above Wild Horse Creek and, *I* was appalled when I saw the bull, a little black fellow only about 2/3 the size of Bessie! He took his duties seriously and proceeded with the encounter. Bad news! He wasn't tall enough to reach the target and after several efforts, seemed to be getting rather angry! I wanted to leave! Bob said "No" and since we didn't have a platform for the bull to stand on, we would have to lead Bessie to a ditch. That way, Bob said, the bull could stand on higher ground and the trajectory could be adjusted! I thought Bob was nuts! We led Bessie around, with the bull becoming more and more irritated until Bob found the elevation which he thought would work. After a few tries, and some guiding help from Bob, the encounter was completed! I was amazed at how small his equipment was as compared to the Hereford's but Bessie didn't seem to mind! Apparently the encounter "took" as Bessie's attempts at riding ceased and in the proper time, she delivered a beautiful calf. It appeared, to me, that size was not that important. It was a comforting thought!

***

The year 1939 continued to be filled with happenings, both at home and overseas. On September 1st, Hitler, that "good man", had his troops invade Poland. England and France declared war on Germany several days later, setting off World War 2! The war still seemed far away to America and a great majority of our citizens felt strongly that we should not get involved. Congress had passed the 1935 Neutrality Act which actually prevented us from giving aid to any country. Prominent leaders in Congress and Government protested any effort to lend assistance. One of those protesting loudly was Joseph Kennedy, the father of one of our future presidents!

In the fall of 1939, Aunt Annie visited us and repeated her offer, to send one of us to high school, if we would stay with her in Jennings. No one had accepted her offer before and since I would graduate from grade school in the spring, it was my turn to consider her offer. It was an opportunity which was not available to us in Chesterfield at that time. The nearest high school was in Eureka, Mo., about 30 miles away, with no means of transportation to get there. In addition, at that time, the school had a poor reputation. I was very much interested in continuing my education and, after talking with Mom, accepted Aunt Annie's offer.

Events moved quickly in Europe in early 1940, as Germany captured Belgium, Denmark, Luxemburg, Norway and the Netherlands. In June, the Germans moved into France and, that once great nation fell the same month! In the U.S.A.,

President Roosevelt was elected to his third term, after defeating Wendell Wilke, pushed his promised "New Deal" and ordered aid to England and Russia by way of shipments of food and medical supplies through the Red Cross. England was taking a pounding and their outlook was grim! General Pershing, of World War I fame, strongly urged our assistance, while stating that the Allies were engaged in a fight for civilization. At this same time, an estimated 85% of our citizens were opposed to our intervention. We still had over 5 million unemployed; minimum wage was 40 cents per hour, and the country seemed more interested in the 1939 and 1940 World's Fair in New York than the problems in Europe! Our government continued to sell scrap iron to Japan, who manufactured war material which they used in their continuing war with China. In 1940, the U.S.A. had only a volunteer army consisting of 75,000 men. When an army unit was moved to a new base in Kansas, the students at our school were dismissed, to watch the convoy as it traveled slowly West along highway 40/61. It was the first time that we saw any tanks or army equipment and we were impressed! Actually, our tanks, guns and equipment, at that time, were already obsolete!

I graduated from the Chesterfield school in May, along with my five classmates, and the six of us were ready to take on the world! We really didn't think that the war would last very long and doubted that our country would ever be involved. The events which followed, month after month, altered our thinking!

President Roosevelt finally succeeded in getting a "Lend Lease" bill approved, and our factories began producing material for shipment to England and Russia. Employment increased and the country's future brightened!

***

I went to stay with Aunt Annie about the last of August, to be ready for my first day of high school. Aunt Annie gave me the choice of the Jennings Public School or McBride's all boy's school, taught by the Catholic order of "The Society of Mary". I chose McBride and the choice was a good one! I was immediately impressed by the knowledge and dedication of the teaching Brothers and I had great respect for them. I will always remember a comment made by our home room teacher, during our first week of school. Someone brought up the war in Europe and the crushing of France's "Maginot Line", just a short time before. The Brother expressed his views: "You will all be in a world war conflict before this is over! Without U.S.A. aid, Britain will succumb, after fighting bravely! France was a country of "OLD MEN" and I expected them to fall immediately! The "Maginot Line" was obsolete, but they based their defense on it, rather than personal strength. When I say "OLD MEN", I don't mean old by years, but by WILL! France had become obsessed by sex, sports, food and personal pleasures and no longer had any will to fight as men! Pray that the same does not happen to our country!" The good Brother was more of a prophet than we could have realized! I wonder what he would say, if he were here today!

I was more than a little anxious about life in the city, not knowing my way around, the attitude of city students and the male Catholic Brothers as teachers, but I soon adjusted to my new environment. When assigned to my homeroom, I learned that I was the only student who had not attended a Catholic grade school. I thought that this may prove to be an obstacle, but I managed to do as well or better than most, obtaining complimentary grades in all subjects. I was surprised at how much more mature the country students were than their city counterparts. I guess, many from our Chesterfield area were exposed to a harder life and just grew up faster! I was always anxious to get home on weekends, since I missed our entire family.

Hitler invaded Russia in 1940 and in September our government instituted the first "Peace Time Draft" to increase our military strength. Those drafted would serve one year and then be discharged. Of course, it didn't work out that way!

Mary got a job at Old Trails Inn, a restaurant in Gumbo, and worked there for a short time. Everything seemed to move faster now, and more talk of war was being heard. Our factories were increasing their production of military materials and new civilian products were appearing in our markets. General Electric had a free demonstration of "Things of the Future", which they held in a large tent in Forest Park. Since I could purchase a student bus pass for 75cents a week, which entitled me to unlimited bus use, I attended their exhibit. It was impressive as they demonstrated the first television set, synthetic materials, nylon stockings and many other inventions. When they told of clothing being made from synthetics, using items such as cow's milk, the audience really laughed! Little did we realize that the astounding articles we witnessed then would be the ordinary in some years in the future.

I got an "after school job" of filling oil heating stoves for the Real Estate Office, the Justice of the Peace Office and the Barber Shop, all located in one building at Jennings Road and McLaren Ave. I filled them each night during the week, from oil drums stored in a supply building at the rear of the offices. My pay was 75 cents a week and they paid me every other week.

Mom insisted that she give me $1.00 each week, for transportation and what ever else I needed. I generally skipped school lunch or would buy only a bowl of chili, in McBride's cafeteria, for 5 cents. The maximum *I* spent for lunches each week would be 25 cents. From Mom's $1.00 and my 75 cent earnings, after purchasing my weekly bus pass for 75 cents, *I* had 75 cents left for anything else. On weekends, *I* used my pass to get to the Delmar Loop, then take a bus to Creve Coeur for 25 cents and hitch a ride to Chesterfield.

Joe sold his 1932 Ford and bought a 1936 Ford sedan from the Fortman girl for $200.00. It was a really nice 2 door V/8 gray sedan, in good shape. Boo bought a 1934 Ford 2 door black sedan. It was a good looking auto, in good shape, also. Both remained in the family and provided a lot of transportation for a long time

New automobiles were introduced each fall and some excitement always surrounded each model as they were unveiled. On a return from a high school game with some friends, we stopped at the Toddle House, on Kings Highway, for a hamburger. After our burgers, we crossed the street to await a North bound bus. The bus stop was right in front of Auffenberg Ford and they had a 1940 model Ford on display in their shop window. We were peering through the window, when a night janitor saw us, came out and invited us inside to see the car. We were impressed. He told us, that since this was a 1940 model and the new ones were already out, the company would sell this black coupe for about $600.00 It was a beautiful car but we all realized that we would probably never have enough money to own a car like that!

***

At home, Old Buck White had died and his wife, Liza, moved into the city with one of her family, leaving their little shack, at the base of our hill, vacant. It wasn't vacant very long, when someone burned it down. We always suspected that the

Steiners may have burned the house down to prevent another black family from occupying it. There were a number of people who were quite prejudiced against blacks and we could never understand their narrowness. Pop always tried to help any of the black families any way he could.

Although the White's shack was no longer there, the charred rocks and lonesome remaining cactus created a spooky area, and we could imagine that "Old Buck" was still guarding "his place!" One week end, just at dark, Joe, Pop and I stood looking down in the valley where the White's shack once stood, and Joe began speculating that Old Buck's ghost was still around! Of course, Pop added to Joe's remarks, that ghosts nearly always came back around, after their old home was burned! I said I didn't believe that and I wasn't afraid of Old Buck's ghost! Joe then offered to give me 50 cents if I would go down to the site and bring back a rock from the burned area. I agreed to go! Joe then changed his requirement. He said that I should light a match and hold it up when I reached the site, so that he could see it.

He then warned that Old Buck was likely to keep blowing the match out. With that, I had some second thoughts, but since I knew that Joe was doing everything to protect his 50 cents and I sure wanted that 50 cents, I went, reached the site, retrieved the rock and, with trembling hands, struck a match! If the match would have been blown out or if someone said, "Get off my place, this is my place now", I probably would have died on the spot! No time was lost in my return to our house on the hill and Joe reluctantly paid me the 50 cents. Pop delighted in telling ghost stories and told them to our black neighbors when ever the opportunity presented itself. If any came to borrow kerosene or sugar shortly before dark, Pop would start and continue his ghost stories to well after dark. Our neighbors were often then afraid to go home. Pop always made certain that his description of "ghost paths" always matched those paths necessary to travel in reaching their homes! Joe liked to scare us also, but I think that he often scared himself as much, when he tried!

***

I signed up for the McBride boxing team and trained at the boxing gym at Sherman Park, on Cote Brilliant, across from McBride. The building is no longer there. Our trainer, a retired professional boxer, had us work hard at our training, since he wanted us qualified for our early spring matches. I was in the flyweight division and drew my first opponent. Amateur fights only go for three rounds and we all felt confident of our skills. I was awarded a T.K.O. in the 2nd round when the referee stopped the fight. My friends said that I was good, and I made the mistake of believing them! I had never seen my next opponent fight, but some of my friends had, and they assured me that it would be an easy victory for me. They told me that he fought with both hands high near his head, leaving his stomach completely exposed. I was confident and invited Aunt Annie and family to witness my upcoming victory! The big night came and all were in attendance. When the first bell rang and we left our corners, I noticed that my friends were correct, he held both hands high, near his head, and left his stomach wide open. I tried a few left jabs at his head then drop my body slightly to fire a hard right to his stomach! As I scored a hard stomach punch, he delivered a powerful left and right to my head! This maneuver was repeated many times and, he literally beat the heck out of me! His stomach must have been like iron, but my eyes and jaw were not. I was happy to hear the final bell and was not the least surprised when he was awarded all three rounds! I fought one exhibition fight, after that, and then turned in my gloves. My boxing career was short lived!

PART TWO
CLOUDS OF WAR AND THE REAL THING

***

Boo, Joe and Ferd had all registered for the draft and, following their physical exams, were classified. Boo and Joe were both classified 1-A, but Ferd was rejected, due to his ear injury. The doctor told Ferd that he would never enter the army. How wrong he turned out to be!

Since Ferd was told that he would not be called, he purchased a beautiful 1941 Ford Club Coupe. I think it cost him a little over $800.00. It was light blue and a real beauty, the first new car that anyone of our family owned. The purchase proved to be a wise one since, no new automobiles were produced after the 1941 models until after the war ended.

Boo was called in the first draft and entered Fort Leonard Wood in May, for his basic training. In the same month, a U.S. Merchant ship, the "Robin Moore", was sunk by a German U Boat in the North Atlantic. The war was beginning to touch some American lives! Japanese and American relations were deteriorating and finally the scrap metal sales to them were halted and, in July, the U.S.A. froze all Japanese assets in this country. Joe was drafted in August and we expected both he and Boo to be back home the following year. It would be more than four years before we saw Joe again, since he never received one furlough in all the time he served.

When Boo completed Basic Training at Fort Leonard Wood, visitors were allowed on Sunday. Ferd offered to drive us up in his new Ford. Pop, Tom, Ferd and I went and the ride seemed to take a long time, since the highways were not designed for fast flowing traffic and no "super highways" existed. We were following an older Buick on an uphill grade, when the Buick stopped suddenly. Ferd couldn't stop completely in time, and the front of his new car was damaged! We were all sick about that! The damage was not too serious, though, and we continued to the army camp, found Boo and visited for several hours before returning home.

I re-entered McBride in September, the same month that the U.S. Destroyer, "Greer" was attacked by a German U Boat. This attack occurred shortly after Roosevelt and Churchill met and signed the "Allied Agreement". It seemed that we may be eventually drawn into the conflict!

Mr. and Mrs. Condict, their son Buddy, daughter Marquita and nephew Barton White, rented the Haeussler farm, occupied their dwelling and became our new neighbors on the hill. Mrs. Condict wanted help with the household chores and Mary went to work for them. In November, Ferd and Loretta were married, and Ferd built a small house on Wild Horse Creek Road. He didn't expect to enter the military draft.

***

I continued to admire the teaching Brothers and recognized the contributions their efforts made in developing well adjusted young men for the future. After expressing an interest to learn more about their order, Brother Martin encouraged me to join. After much prayerful consideration and discussion with Mom, I decided that it would be a rewarding vocation and agreed to enter the seminary novitiate the day after Christmas, 1941. This would be at the Christmas break in the seminary and at the end of the semester at McBride.

On Sunday morning, December 7, 1941, I attended early mass with Aunt Annie, and met Elmer Vieth and his father, Bill, on the way out of church. Elmer told me that his dad had purchased a new shotgun and asked if I would like to go with them to test it out. We would be back shortly after noon. I agreed to go. We went to an abandoned farm, owned by Uncle Phil, near where Central City now stands. We fired the shotgun at clay birds, walked over the farm and visited. Upon our return, we took Bill Vieth home and were met by his wife at their door. She was very excited! She said the Japanese had bombed Pearl Harbor and the news was on the radio! We looked at each other as Elmer asked, "Where is Pearl Harbor?" I said that I thought it was on the coast of California. How little we all knew of the world in which we would all soon be quite familiar. The news reported that several ships were damaged or sunk and an unknown number of people killed. When the actual facts were known, the bulk of our naval fleet was destroyed and over 2400 Americans killed! Roosevelt announced that we declared war on Japan and the following day declared war on the Axis Powers. We were now in the full blown war!

Christmas day was spent at the farm. It would be my last visit home for a long while since the seminary permitted only a short two week vacation in the summer and visits from family on one Sunday of each month. When I went to say goodbye to Pop, he reluctantly shook hands as he said, "I'd rather see you going in the goddam army!" I was crushed! I had just turned 15 years of age a few days before and it would be at least 2 years before I could even enlist in the navy! I wanted Pop to be proud of me, also, but I think that was a long time in coming!

The day after Christmas, Rita Deuser and Aunt Annie drove me to McBride High, where we picked up Brother Martin, and then to Maryhurst Seminary on Lindberg Blvd. in Kirkwood. After a short tour and introductions, they left and I began my first day of seminary life. I was surprised that only a few novitiates were in attendance and my classes would consist of only three or four students. All in all, there were too few students for a good soccer game, and we had to enlist several priests and brothers when we had that recreation. I learned that we would have two more courses than the McBride schedule, one of which was French. The other novices already had a full semester of French, so I would be starting a full three months behind them and have to catch up. I was determined to put forth my best effort and accepted the schedule and tasks with enthusiasm.

Some of the policies in the seminary were strange, however, and I still find difficulty in trying to understand their reasoning in instituting them. The places at the table were assigned and rotated counter clockwise daily, with the person at the head of the table charged with slicing the home made bread. Since, at my first meal, I sat one chair to the right of the head place; my second day placed me at the head of the table. All meals were taken in silence and anyone requesting bread would do so in a quiet whisper. It seemed that each time I started to eat, someone would ask for bread. After a number of such interruptions I decided to slice the entire loaf. No further requests for bread were made! When I was nearly finished, the priest quietly whispered to me that it was required that I eat any sliced bread which was not requested! There was nearly 2/3 of the loaf left, but I ate it, while questioning in my mind, why that policy was not whispered to me before I sliced all of the bread! About a week later, our evening meal included cooked, or I should say partly cooked turnips, since the centers remained raw. I took a reasonable helping and the Prefex suggested that I take more. I thanked him, in a whisper, but said I was not overly fond of cooked turnips. With that, he took the entire bowl and dumped them on my plate! I ate the turnips, said no more, but was learning the hard way!

Seminaries, at that time, were very strict and no radio, newspapers or magazines were allowed. All outgoing and incoming mail was censored, as were any books to be read. News of the war and the world, in limited quantity, was given to us verbally by our Prefex. I missed knowing what was happening in the war and anxious for current data on my brothers in service. Ferd was re-classified and inducted into the army in January, 1942. Boo and Joe were already overseas in the South Pacific, and the news we received of our country's losses was discouraging!

After Ferd entered the army, Loretta got a job at Carter Carburetor, in St. Louis and was later instrumental in getting Mary a job there, also. Mary then found a home, near the plant, where she could have room and board with a nice older couple. She then could stay in the city during the week and come home on weekends. Mary would continue at that job for a number of years.

Life at the seminary was very structured, so that little time was left for personal activity. So called "free time" was limited to several hours on Thursday afternoon and Sunday afternoon. This free time could be used to write letters, read or do homework, but was often taken up with lengthy walks. One of my classmates, a boy from Detroit, a few years older than I was, proved a real friend in helping me learn the many rules and preventing me from violating ones, with which I had not been made aware. Several of the others seemed to experience some pleasure when I did something wrong! My friend occupied the bunk next to mine, and taught me how to make up the bunk, dress and still meet the bell in the short time allotted to these functions. I considered him to be a model seminarian and appreciated his help. Upon being awakened at the bell, one morning, I was shocked to see that the bunk which he occupied , when we retired, was made up and he was no where to be seen! He had left during the night after we had all gone to bed, which, as I later learned, was the policy employed if you wished to discontinue your novitiate! From that point, all seemed downhill for me and the structured environment began to depress me! I really enjoyed the Easter visit by our family, including Mom, Sis, Ed and kids, but after that Sunday, I realized that I would not continue this life! I wrote a letter to Mom, asking her to have Bob drop off my suitcase. The letter, of course, was censored and, I was instructed to say nothing to anyone and leave quietly when the suitcase arrived. I did, but before leaving I managed to say good bye to my favorite teacher, Brother Edwin Kramer, who had tears in his eyes as he shook my hand and wished me luck! He and I planted over 50 hard maple trees on the seminary grounds on Lindberg, where a shopping center and Catholic girl school now stand. Mary and a boy friend picked me up and I returned to a world, which, after such a short absence, seemed quite strange!

Back at the farm, I tackled chores with vigor, spending the first several days hauling horse manure, with the team and sled, from the barn lot to a field southeast of the house. I was depressed and discouraged for having been unable to accept the novitiate life and considered my efforts to be a failure! While mentally reviewing the events of the past months, however, I recalled the words of Brother Edwin, when I told him of my failures. He said, "Ray, if you have given your best efforts to any undertaking, it is no disgrace to fail! The disgrace is when you refuse to pick yourself up and start again! THERE IS BUT ONE MATTER IN WHICH WE CANNOT AFFORD TO FAIL, AND THAT IS THE SALVATION OF YOUR SOUL! THERE IS NO SECOND CHANCE, AND ETERNITY IS FOREVER!" I'll always remember the words of this fine man!

When I had been home about one week, Aunt Annie came out and told me that the principal at McBride had called and asked me to return to school. He said he understood how I may feel, and I could return to my old home room or choose a new room. In either event, should I accept and return he assured me that no student would ever mention my entering or leaving Maryhurst. I accepted, returned to my old home room class and, everyone treated me as though I had never been gone! I discovered that I was far advanced of our class in lessons, and completed the year with no problems.

***

Pop got a job for me that summer, at Spackler's farm, which was across from Ferd's house on Wild Horse Creek Road. I weeded flower beds, planted trees, flowers, mowed grass, trimmed and was paid $2.00 per day. I was very happy with the work! An old German fellow, named Herman, worked there the year around and I found him to be a real character. At that time, we suspected everyone with a German accent, to be a spy, and those who always said that "Hitler was a good man" were now quite silent!

The summer was busy and news from Boo, Joe and Ferd were always eagerly anticipated. Boo and Joe were already in the South Pacific, Ferd was still in the states, but was later sent to the Yukon Territories and Alaska where the Alcan Highway supply route was being constructed. Bob, Tom and I kept up with the farm chores during the week. On weekends Bob and I spent a number of outings with Mary and some of the new friends which she met through her work at Carter. We had some enjoyable times. Saturday nights were special dance nights at an Inn on 40/61 near Hilltown, where Nichol's orchestra would whip out some circle dances and the Rombach family enjoyed their well deserved recreation by consuming large amounts of beer. We also got to know our new neighbors, Buddy and Marquita Condict and their cousin Barton White. Bob spent a good bit of time with them and wanted to get better acquainted with Marquita!

I started my junior year at McBride, in September, and began looking for an "after school" job. The $2.00 per day earned at Spacklers during part of the summer, increased my desire for a little more spending money. I really was hoping for a job at a service station, pumping gas and cleaning up, but jobs were scarce and competition was keen. When Uncle Phil heard that I was interested in finding some part time work, he discouraged the filling station approach and suggested that I apply at The North Side Bank, since he understood that they may be interested in some additional help. I stopped at the bank after school, the next day, knocked at the closed door, and was met by Bill Sertl, who let me in, chatted a while, then introduced me to Ed Jezik, who would teach me the bookkeeping operation. I began work the next day on October 2, 1942. They would pay me 25 cents per hour and I would work after school, Friday nights, Saturdays and during school and vacation holidays. Although the entire bookkeeping and miscellaneous bank functions were foreign to me, I was excited about learning and grateful for the job.

The bank was small, with a total staff of seven people, including me. Webe H Naunheim Sr. was president, and I immediately recognized and appreciated the warmth and consideration he had for the bank and the entire staff. The group worked closely together in all matters and was truly a family type unit. Banking was far different from what is known today, in that nearly all functions were completed by hand, which resulted in long, tedious hours on many peak days! Accuracy was paramount and it was rare when an error occurred in any customer transaction.

***

On Thanksgiving day, at the farm that fall, Bob suggested that he, Buddy Condict and I take the shotguns and walk the creek, with the prospect of bagging a few stray mallards. We met Buddy and started at our property, planning to work slowly upstream along the bank. Ducks would often settle down in pools near a bend or under some overhanging root snags. Just upstream from our property, we came upon a small flock, which swung wide, out of range, and flew downstream. Since ducks would often fly back upstream when flushed a second time, we agreed that I would stay on our property, while Bob and Buddy moved downstream to search for the ducks. If flushed, they would then have an opportunity to shoot and I would also, if the ducks flew upstream. Bob and Buddy started across the field to intercept the flock downstream. I had Pop's single barrel 12 gauge shotgun loaded with BB size shot, for greater knockdown power and range. I crossed the stream on a log and selected a spot behind a large sycamore tree, which leaned far out over the stream. Some of the roots of the sycamore tree were exposed and stood a foot or so above the ground. After Bob and Buddy were gone for a short while, I decided to shift my position so that I could stand on the root structure for better vision and concealment. While holding the shotgun in my right hand, I reached for a limb above me with my left hand and placed my right foot on the root snag. When I put weight on my right foot, it slipped from mud on the soles of my boot and, somehow, the gun slipped from my grasp! There was a blinding flash, an ear splitting roar and the smell of gun powder filled my nostrils! I felt my chin and head, knowing that part of me would be gone! It all seemed to be there! In looking down at my jacket, I couldn't believe what I saw! Before we started out that morning, I looked for a jacket to wear and found Boo's suede jacket, which he left when he entered the service. I wore it, even though it was much too large and loose fitting. Now, as I looked down, the zipper remained together for about six inches from the bottom, and then was torn out nearly to the top of my chest, where a hole was blown through! I carefully removed the jacket and then noticed where some pellets had gone through the left collar! Powder and shot left darkened grooves on my white sweat shirt, from just above my navel to the top of my chest! I still couldn't believe what had happened! The gun was not cocked, but he hammer must have struck a root as the gun fell and fired! I was leaning out, in line with the tree, and apparently the oversize jacket was extended from my body when the gun discharged. I opened the breech and looked at the spent casing, still unwilling to believe what had happened! I put the jacket back on, crossed the creek and stood waiting as Bob and Buddy returned. "Did you get one?" Bob asked as they approached. "Almost!" was my reply. Bob and Buddy were then near enough to see the jacket, and the color drained from Bob's face! "My God, what happened?" I told them! We agreed to say nothing to Mom and, when we reached the house, I hung Boo's ruined jacket on a nail in the garage, just southeast of the house. It stayed there until the farm was sold and Mom never learned of this strange accident. If you believe in miracles, I know that one happened that day! God must have had some other purpose to allow me to continue my existence! I mentally recreated that event many times and concluded that, there was no natural way the blast could have missed me, and yet, I had not a single scratch!

School work and bank training continued and I began to develop some speed and skill in operating the bookkeeping machine. Accuracy and speed were both critical and I was satisfied with my progress in both.

***

In early December, something happened, which eventually developed into the most important part of my entire life! Upon leaving mass, one Sunday morning at Corpus Christi Church, I noticed a young girl coming down the steps and walk. She had an energetic walk, pretty smile and teeth and a mischievous twinkle in her eyes. I smiled and said, "Hi!" as she passed, and she returned the smile and greeting! I had to find out who she was and then had to meet her! No one seemed to know! After listening to my description of this girl, a number of times, my cousin Rita Deuser said that she had to be Jane Hanebrink. I looked up the Hanebrink phone number and made a call. When a man answered, whom I assumed to be Jane's father, I asked to speak to Jane. A gruff, unfriendly voice responded, "There ain't no Jane here!", and hung up. I got the wrong Hanebrink. I didn't want to risk that again, realizing that she wouldn't know who I was, if I called, I decided on another approach. I purchased 25 Christmas cards with my name imprinted and, after verifying the address for the correct Hanebrinks, mailed one of the cards to Jane. I expected and received no response, but I felt that curiosity would cause her to find out who I was, and when I finally met and introduced myself, she would remember the name.

When school classes continued, after the Christmas holidays, I found that we had a new chemistry teacher. Chemistry was not one of my favorite subjects and I found more difficulty in following this change of teachers. I was not doing well in the subject and was a bit discouraged. About the second week in January, when I reported for work at the bank, after school, Mr. Naunheim called me into his office. He said that the bank was growing, that they need to have some full time help and would I be interested in the job? It would mean leaving school, but he thought we could work out a satisfactory arrangement to continue my education. He had served on the faculty at the St. Louis University, where he taught a course in "Commerce and Finance" for a number of years, and knew the members of the staff and those in admissions. He felt that I could later pick up courses at the University which would be to my advantage. After talking to Uncle Phil and Aunt Annie, I accepted his offer, left school the following week and became a full time, permanent employee of the bank. My new full time salary would be $100.00 per month. Yes, I became a "high school drop out", that which I am not proud and would

strongly advise anyone to never drop out of school. I always regretted the absence of my McBride diploma! Mr. Naunheim's intentions were good, and he had several conversations with St. Louis University. My formal credentials were inadequate for acceptance, however, and even had they been, it is doubtful that I could have paid the required fees and tuition. A long educational struggle followed through the succeeding years, which consisted of many self taught courses from books, nine years of night classes in specific law and banking courses, and some personal tutoring from Mr. Naunheim. Little could I have dreamed, at that time, that a non-diploma high school drop out would eventually become President and Chief Executive

Officer of this very bank, and that I would retire from my banking career in February, 1987, after serving my last five years as Chairman of the Board and Chief Executive Officer of the Charter Bank of Webster Groves, the second largest bank in the Charter group!

***

An announcement appeared in the church bulletin, of a school dance to be held at the Corpus Christi Hall on February 26, 1943. I felt certain that Jane would be there and I planned to attend. It was on a Friday night, and I would not finish work until about 8:00 P.M., at about the same time the dance started. It was a bit after 8:00 when I left the bank and walked the few blocks to the hall. The floor was crowded and efforts to locate Jane were not successful. I feared that she may not have come! I climbed to the balcony to look over the crowd and saw a pretty girl on the far side of the hall. Jane was there! She was wearing a green sweater and a grey skirt. As I started down the stairs to meet her, sirens began a continuous wail, and shortly all lights went out! It was a practice blackout drill to prepare in the event of a bombing raid! The drill lasted about 15 minutes and I located Jane when the lights went on again. After introductions and friendly chatter, in which she introduced a friend from high school, who would be spending the weekend, a cute little girl named Mickey Verner. A friend of mine, Gene Gehm, was also at the dance and was introduced to Mickey. Gene and I persuaded the girls to let us walk them home. It was an exciting evening and I knew that I wanted to see more of Jane Hanebrink!

***

I had purchased a small motor scooter and rode it out to the farm several times. It lacked power to climb the hill to our house but I managed by walking alongside while running the engine. On occasion when I rode the scooter to work, at the bank, Mr. Naunheim insisted that I bring it inside for safety. I then parked it in an unused office, off the lobby, in the front section of the bank. It leaked a little gasoline, leaving the fumes drifting around the bank. I felt embarrassed and wanted to again move it outside, but Mr. Naunheim insisted that it was no problem and should remain in the unused office. I felt badly about the gasoline fumes and stopped riding the scooter to the bank!

***

After several telephone calls to Jane, we agreed on a date for a Sunday afternoon at the Fox Theatre, on Grand Avenue, to see a popular movie. Admission would be 50 cents each to attend this classy theatre but this was an important date and I wanted to impress Jane. Her parents had planned a family gathering for that evening and wanted Jane to be home before dark. The theatre was crowded and a long wait was necessary before we were admitted. At about the half way point in the movie, I realized that we would have to leave, if we were to meet Jane's parents return time. We left by an exit on the balcony of the Fox, only to learn, as the Exit door locked behind us, that we were on a fire escape about 3 stories above the street. We descended to the last level of the fire escape, which ended about 10 feet above the alley! A door to the building, on this level, was unlocked and we entered the building. A semi-darkened stairs led to the basement and we finally found our way to the street! The bus ride home seemed to take longer than it should, but we arrived within the designated time frame requested. Jane's parents, when learning that we didn't stay for the movie, told us that we certainly should have, and they would have understood if we had been late.

I purchased special tickets for the live theatre, for our fourth date, and bought a pretty gardenia corsage for Jane. It was a beautiful evening and provided the atmosphere for an affirmative answer when I asked for our first good night kiss. Jane said "No!" I was disappointed and described my feelings later, to Bob. "You damned fool!" Bob said, "You never ask a girl for a kiss, you just take it!" I had a lot of respect for Bob and his knowledge of such things and decided that approach would be employed! Bob, his date, Jane and I doubled on our seventh date. Bob had Boo's car and we were on our way to a movie by way of Goodfellow Blvd. and West Florissant Avenue. At the first intersection, I followed Bob's instructions and "took" my first kiss from Jane! She called me a "dirty rat!" The twinkle in her eyes betrayed her, however, and I knew that she liked the kiss!

Jane and I spent many summer afternoons with Bob, Mary, their dates and friends, in Forest Park, picnics and movies. We had an enjoyable summer. I was anxious to show Jane our old hill farm and introduce her to Mom, Pop and Tom. When we visited the farm, I wanted to share our country knowledge with Jane, show her the honey bee trees, the fox den along the bank of the creek and how to smell copperhead snakes! She was interested in everything, but questioned our ability to smell copperheads! I told her that there were many things, in the hill country, that were true but hard to believe! I told her that on a still, hot summer night, if you stand quietly in the center of a corn field, YOU CAN HEAR THE CORN GROW! She didn't believe it! I offered to take her to the corn field to prove it but she said she wasn't about to go into a cornfield with me at night to "Listen to the corn grow!" She never did!

***

The bank was open until noon on Saturdays and it would

generally be around 2:30 before everything was balanced and we could leave, resulting in a short weekend. Although gasoline and tires were rationed, I really wanted to have an automobile and checked out any possibilities that came along. A bank customer who operated a service station, told me that he had purchased a 1935 Ford sedan from one of his customers and that I could have it for $175.00. I arranged for a loan through the bank and bought the car. I had to install a heater, which cost $20.00, and I was on wheels! Gasoline rationing only allowed several gallons of gasoline per week under the basic "A" permit and I needed more. I applied for a "B" sticker which would allow me enough to get home on weekends. My application stated the fact that three of my brothers were already in service and the fourth brother was scheduled to enter soon, and I wanted to go home on weekends to visit my parents. The others at the bank said that I wouldn't get the "B" sticker and all were surprised when I did! Mine was the only auto at the bank with a "B" sticker. Jane's dad had an "A" sticker for his 1941 Plymouth and a "T" sticker for his farm truck. The "T" sticker allowed a purchase of at least 10 gallons of gasoline a week.

The 1935 Ford was not a very good one, but at least it was transportation and I appreciated having it. Bob, in the meanwhile, was having tire problems with Boo's 1934 Ford, so he improvised with a method somewhat hard to believe today. He took some old tires, cut out a section, and inserted them in the existing tires to serve as a continuous boot! After inflating the inner tube, the boot left a small space, creating a continuous "thump"! It was noisy and a little rough riding, but it worked!

***

Pop got a job at the TNT plant near Weldon Springs and the home financial picture was improving. Mom and Pop felt that they could finally complete the house by replacing the shed section with two bedrooms and a room for a future bath. Bob, along with brothers in law, Wayne and Ed, tore off the shed section and built the additional rooms. It was a great addition and Mom was pleased but had one complaint. The floor wasn't level! Mom said that you could place a marble on the floor and it would roll to the outside wall! When Boo returned home, after the war, he inspected the new addition and commented on the slightly sloping floor. When electricity became available, Mom said that they planned to complete the improvements. The farm was sold before any additional improvements were made, but Mom finally got her electricity and bath in a new house built after the war.

I don't know how Pop managed all the strength and energy that he seemed to have! His job at the TNT involved laying out and building roads, and after working a full shift, would sometimes have to walk all the way home from Weldon Springs, a distance of over seven miles! Pop was all muscle and not an ounce of fat!

***

In October 1943, as we all arrived for our Sunday mass at Ascension Church, we were met at the door by Father Godfrey. Father was visibly upset and he said that he had some very bad news! Eddie Musterman had an accident with his car and died from burns and injuries! We were shocked and deeply saddened! That morning mass seemed a blur to me as I thought of Ed, Sis and family! After dinner, that day, Bob and I went down to one of our rented fields where Bob had field corn cut and shocked. We shucked a wagon load of corn while talking of Ed's death and the hardships which Sis and family would have to face. Our hearts were heavy, as we realized that there was little that we could do to help! Ed, somehow seemed indestructible, and his death was hard to accept! I later drove out Lucas and Hunt Road to the site where the accident occurred. Ed had some carburetor problems with his 1937 Packard and carried a container of gasoline on the floor behind his seat. At a sharp curve on Lucas and Hunt Road, his front tire blew out and the car went out of control, hitting an electric pole. The auto burst into flame and the gasoline container ignited, trapping Ed inside! He was pulled from the burning wreck by a black truck driver, but died from his injuries later that night! I commend Sis, our nephew and nieces, for their devotion to each other and the great efforts made by all of them in their struggle to overcome this tragedy!

**

The road work was nearly completed at the TNT plant and Pop was offered a job at Kingsport, Tennessee, at a site which would later be known as the site where some of Atomic Bomb components were produced. With this possibility, and the realization that Bob would also soon be in service, Pop told me that he and Mom decided to sell the farm. It would be impossible for Mom and Tom to maintain the property alone. Pop thought that I might know someone, through the bank connection, who would be interested. He said the 39 plus acres, with several hundred fruit trees, a spring fed creek, house, barn and improvements in Chesterfield, should be worth $5,000.00. Several doctors and a dentist had previously indicated to me that they were looking for such a place and I told them of Pop's decision to sell. I couldn't get anyone to even look at the property since they all said that $5,000.00 was too much money! It wasn't until after the war that Mom and Pop sold, all but two acres at the bottom of the hill, for $7,000.00. Property in the Chesterfield area now sells for at least $50,000.00 per acre!

Bob had wanted to join the service for some time, but Mom wanted him to stay home as long as he could. As 1944 began, however, Bob and I discussed going into the service together, since I had now passed my 17th birthday and could enlist in the Navy. I was surprised when, on a Saturday night outing with Bob, he told me that he had joined the marines! "The MARINES, why did you do a thing like that?" I asked. It seemed that Bob had an argument with a girl friend and decided to get even with her. "Boy, you sure showed her!"

I wondered why he didn't pick a gentler branch, but he must have been pretty angry with that girl. I think Bob did the suffering, however, rather than the girl he intended to punish! We realized now that the services would no longer permit members of the same family to serve together. This policy was adopted when the five Sullivan brothers were all killed when the ship on which they were serving was lost.

Bob entered the Marines in March and I decided to join the Merchant Marine. The Merchant Marine had lost a considerable number of seamen and ships, especially in the early stages of the war, and was now actively advertising for men, since all Merchant Marine service was strictly voluntary. At war end the total loss of Merchant Seamen's lives by enemy action was more than 6000 men with the loss of 733 Merchant ships. Many thousands more were wounded and nearly 600 made prisoners of war. I felt strongly to be a part of that service so I contacted the U.S. Maritime Commission and obtained the necessary data for enlistment. In June, I passed my physical and was sworn in at St. Louis. I sold my 1935 Ford to a friend for $195.00, which recovered my original cost plus the heater. Another friend in St. Louis finally sold my motor scooter, so I had money in the bank as I began my Maritime adventure.

Before my scheduled departure, Ferd was transferred back to the states from Alaska for a furlough before being sent to Europe and Bob was home on leave after completing his basic Marine training. Their furloughs ended with Ferd returning on Friday, Bob on Saturday, and my train left for my basic training on Sunday afternoon. After telling Mom and Tom "goodbye" on Sunday morning, I was more than a little disappointed to learn that Pop had left the house, without telling me "goodbye". I'm sure that my disappointment was apparent to Mom as she told me that she saw Pop going to the alfalfa field with a hoe. Realizing that little time remained if I was to reach St. Louis in time for train departure, I ran to the alfalfa field! I saw Pop bent over and chopping vigorously at imaginary weeds with a heavy grubbing hoe. As I drew near, I called, "Pop, I don't have much time, I'll have to hurry to be on time for my train, and *I* wanted to tell you "goodbye". He never looked up but kept chopping at the ground! Thinking that he had not heard me, I called again as I drew within a few yards of him. Still not looking up, he said, "Damn it, be careful! Damn it , be careful! That's all I can say!" It was then that I saw Pop's face, his jaw was tightly set and his cheeks were wet with tears! As I stood there, unable to speak for a moment, I realized that I was looking at a father that I really didn't know before! It was suddenly clear to me, Pop had fought his family's war of the great depression, the war against hunger and poverty, the terrible droughts and the bitter winters of the 1930's, his life having been a continuous battle in wars, in which he had won or was about to win. Now, he watched his greatest possession, his children, go to a war in which he could not fight! In those moments I saw, what I had never seen before, the love and concern he had for all of us! Pop saw each of us return safely from the war and was still on the farm when he died in 1965. I shall never forget that day, in the alfalfa field on the north ridge of our old hill farm, when I gained a better understanding, a greater love and respect for our Pop, who was always the greatest fighter I had ever known.

Irene and Wayne picked up Jane and me, that Sunday afternoon, and took me to Union Station, where our enlistment group was assembled. We were called to attention, our "good-by's" made and we boarded a troop train for California. Five stars were now displayed on the "Service Flag" which hung in the window of our house on the hill.

The first stop for our troop train was Texarkana, Texas, where the train was met by a group of girls handing out apples and wishing us well. We were not allowed off the train, so the girls moved along the tracks, handing apples to us through the open windows. It was a simple and kind gesture and I still have a warm feeling for the residents of that city.

The train laid over, for the better part of the day, in El Paso, Texas, and we were allowed to go into town. Several of us went across the border into Mexico, for a few hours, to see what that Country was like. Not too great!

Our troop train resumed it's slow pace and we finally arrived in Los Angeles, after spending four days and nights on board. We then boarded a bus for Long Beach, then by boat to Avalon, Catalina Island, for our boot training camp. The old Wrigley-Cubs training camp had been converted into the Maritime Service training camp.

The training was similar to all basic boot camps, with emphasis on ship's safety, seamanship and survival. Whale boats were utilized to teach us lifeboat launching, operation, sailing and rescue techniques. Exercises would sometimes take us several miles offshore. All men were given a choice of Deck, Engine or Stewards Department, in which to serve. Those with any physical restrictions, such as vision, were limited to the Stewards Department. I chose the Deck Department since I didn't want to be confined below decks in the engine room, and really wanted the feel and experience of the open sea, above decks. It was a good choice!

I missed Jane and the family and wrote to all of them regularly. I guess that I missed Jane the most, and was sure that I had fallen deeply in love! Her letters came on a regular basis and I always eagerly looked forward to them.

Shortly before completing boot camp, our section was ordered on a training cruise, to become familiar with the workings of a ship and shipboard life. We boarded the ship at Avalon, Catalina, and cruised offshore, up and down the coast for several days. I had my first opportunity to steer the vessel. It was an old ship and sluggish but I was thrilled with anticipation of my first real trip to sea. While on this training cruise, we docked for the weekend at Long Beach and were given our first 2 day pass. I knew that Bob was stationed at Camp Pendleton, for his advanced training, and I started out to find his base and visit him. I hitch hiked to Oceanside and inquired at the main gate to the Marine Base, only to learn that Bob's unit was about 20 miles South on the base. I resumed my hitch hiking and arrived at the road leading back to his camp. I started to walk and was picked up by several marines in a jeep. They told me that it was seven miles to the camp entrance. When we were about 1/4 mile from the entrance, they stopped and explained that I would have to walk the rest of the way, since it was against regulations to accept riders. I thanked them and presented myself to the guard at the entrance. Bob was located in a short time and we visited and exchanged experiences. Bob's unit was scheduled to view some kind of training film that evening, but Bob said that he would fall in for the roll call and then slip out of formation as they left for the film. He said that I should remain quiet, in the tent, until he returned. All went well and Bob returned to the tent for our continued visit. After only a few minutes, however, his C/0 lifted the tent flap, reprimanded Bob, and ordered him to attend the film. I thought that I would have to leave, but Bob suggested that I remain in the tent until he came back and we could visit a bit longer. When Bob returned, we visited until about 10:30 when we said "good-by" and I started back. The seven miles seemed very long and when I finally reached Highway 101 there were several groups of Marines waiting to hitch rides. I knew better than to attempt to join them, and started to walk North on 101. With that, they started to berate and threaten me, calling me "Swabbie" and a few other "not so nice" names. I was dressed in my blue Maritime uniform with a red Maritime insignia, which none of them could recognize. They were a brave lot, standing about ten to my one! I assumed that many had been drinking, to account for their combative behavior. I then walked about 100 yards north and, as I approached several army men hitch hikers, I told them that I was simply going to go past them so that their ride chances would not be at risk. They offered no problem and were courteous. After waiting for about 1/2 hour, a girl driving a 1936 Ford Sedan stopped at the army group and offered them a ride. I made no effort to join them. She then pulled up to me and asked me to get in. With that, the last Marine group started running toward her car. She backed up, yelled that she didn't want them in her car, and then sped off toward Long Beach! I was very grateful and, as I thanked her, the army boys told her of the treatment I had received from the marines. She said that she had some problems with some she had given a ride to before and objected to the attitudes of some. She took us as far as Laguna Beach, where I waited until after 4:00 AM before getting another ride. An old "strange" man gave me a ride up 101 and when I could see the lights of the "Pike" at Long Beach, he turned East on a road leading away from my destination! I asked him to stop and let me out! He refused, saying that this was a short cut to Long Beach! I knew that it was not, and started to mentally review how I was going to tear him up if he tried anything wrong! He didn't, and finally stopped at an intersection and pointed the direction to Long Beach. I walked up the road until I found out that I was in Bell, California. From there I caught a bus back to Long Beach and was back aboard ship at 3:00 PM, two hours before liberty expired. I was mighty tired!

Our basic training was completed; our section split up and sent to various ports where we would be assigned to our first ship. After that first assignment, we would be on our own for all future ships. I was sent to San Francisco, only to learn that the quarters were filled at the assignment barracks. Six of us were then sent to the Alameda Maritime Officers Upgrading School to await assignment. While there, several of us were given a short advanced course in sailing, using a typical lifeboat as our sailing vessel. It was interesting and I enjoyed it. In my free time, I volunteered for a mowing work detail so that I would have something to do.

After about one week, one of the guys in my old section, came to me and excitedly told me that my name and his were posted on the assignment board and that we were to report for duty aboard the S.S. Wisconsin in San Francisco Harbor. The thrill of my first assignment was tarnished, since this boy was probably the dumbest member of our old 60 member section, and I had always hoped to ship out with anyone but him! As he gushed on about being lucky as to being able to ship out with ME, I began to feel a little guilty! It turned out that he was really a nice guy but slow to learn anything. I helped him in any way I could after we were aboard ship. I never saw him again after I left the S.S. Wisconsin.

We arrived at the Wisconsin and went aboard. The ship was an older one, built about 1935, lacked many of the conveniences of the new ships, sailed under the Panamanian flag, under contract to the General Steamship Company and the War Shipping Administration.

It was Sunday when we came aboard and most of the existing crew was ashore. We reported to Chief Mate Richards, who later was made captain. He made it clear that he expected nothing but hard work on his ship and would tolerate nothing short of maximum effort and dedication. He then ordered us on deck to find the bos'n and get to work!

We were assigned to our quarters (focile) and when the days work was finished, settled down for a good sleep. I was awakened about midnight by someone who was shaking me! Startled, I sat up to see a round faced, friendly looking chap with a mischievous grin, asking me if I would like some cold watermelon. The number three hold was refrigerated and the ship was capable of delivering supplies requiring cold temperatures. The stranger introduced himself as DeWayne J. Schwanke, from Minnesota. Thus began an acquaintance which developed into a lifelong period of trust and friendship. The watermelon tasted good!

The S.S. Wisconsin was engaged in running supplies from the states to Pearl Harbor and would travel in convoy with a number of other vessels, escorted by several Navy

Destroyer Escorts. We loaded sugar and pineapple for cargo on the return trip. The sugar was generally picked up in Wailuku, Maui and delivered to Crocker, California, near Sacramento. I made three trips on the S.S. Wisconsin but wanted to get to the South Pacific in the hopes of finding Boo, Joe or Bob. I was determined to check each island where I thought they may be stationed.

While in San Francisco, between voyages on the Wisconsin, I applied for and took the examination for Life Boatman and Able Bodied Seaman Certificate. I passed and was issued the document. A new engine was installed in the one powered lifeboat and Maritime law requires a specified number of hours being run on that engine before it is certified for sea acceptance. Since many of the crew lived in the San Francisco area, and were anxious to be home each evening and on weekends, I was assigned the job of running the necessary hours on the new engine. For an entire week I turned to each morning, cast off with the life boat and cruised around San Francisco Bay. I often went out nearly to the Golden Gate Bridge, cruised near Alcatraz and explored the better part of the bay. I took one of the Navy Armed Guard with me one day and the weather changed when we neared the Golden Gate, resulting in a very rough ride back to the ship. He didn't want to go with me again!

***

When I began my first leave, I learned that the Merchant Marine had no recognition whatever, was not permitted to use the U.S.O. or Red Cross facilities, had no Government life insurance, was unable to obtain private life insurance, had no medical assistance program, paid full fare on all transportation and purchased all their own uniforms and clothing. The wearing of a uniform was optional and few Merchant Seamen wore one. I found without one, however, I was unable to board a train for my trip home, since uniformed personnel were boarded first and the train filled before others had the opportunity to board. After several unsuccessful attempts, I broke out my uniform and made it home.

I spent Christmas 1944 at sea and was surprised on Christmas day, when one of the deck officers presented each member of the crew with a gift consisting of a hand made ditty bag containing a pipe, a tin of tobacco and some hard candy. My bag was made by a group of women in Nova Scotia and the contents were furnished by the Salvation Army. The Salvation Army was the only entity to assist a Merchant Seaman and I have always had a good feeling for that fine organization. I added a few more essentials, such as medical supplies, to my "ditty" bag, attached it to my life preserver, and carried it during the entire time I sailed. I still have it.

***

DeWayne and I agreed to meet at San Pedro after my leave, where we, along with several other friends, Wayne Ulberg and his brother-in-law Tony, would attempt to ship out together. We met as planned, but the opportunity for the four of us to ship together did not-occur. Since my leave had expired and my funds were running low, I was getting anxious and realized that we would have to split up. Reluctantly, I took a single opening for an Able-Bodied Seaman on a T-2 tanker, the S.S. Fort Stevenson, expecting a long trip to the South Pacific, but we went back to Pearl Harbor and returned to San Pedro. I was delighted to find DeWayne, Wayne and Tony back at Wilmington. They had taken an old coastal tanker up the West Coast and returned. They wanted something better and we agreed that all four of us would try to ship together again.

A Liberty ship, the S.S.Frederick Billings, owned by the Alaska Transportation Corporation, under contract to the War Shipping Administration, sent out a request for a complete crew. We jumped at the chance that all of us could be together. DeWayne put in for bos'n, with Wayne, Tony and me filing for Able Seamen. We were all successful and would ship together. When we boarded the S.S. Billings, we soon learned why the ship needed a full crew. Cargo was being moved onto the docks for loading and was stamped "Bent Air". In short order we learned that "Bent Air" was the code name for Calcutta, India, a long trip to a most unattractive place! I was pleased, however, for the opportunity to get to see a country as mysterious and strange as India, and felt that we were fortunate in being able to sail together. We all felt confident in the abilities and dedication of each other. We wondered what our cargo would be, but didn't have to wait long to find out. When the stevedores came aboard as winch operators and loaders, we learned that we would be carrying 8,800 tons of TNT with a deck cargo of trucks, jeeps and equipment. The entire cargo would eventually reach the army units involved in road construction in central and northern India.

When the holds were filled with the cases of TNT, we battened the hatches and prepared for loading the deck cargo. The amount of deck cargo gave the appearance of a top heavy vessel and I wondered how the ship would handle rough weather. After nearly a month at sea, we would find out! Carpenters completed the deck cargo operation by enclosing the entire cargo with plywood and tar paper, all then framed in with 2x6 lumber and then cabled to the deck cleats. A frame catwalk was then built from the officer's deck to the forward section, just aft of the forward gun tub. A wooden ladder was constructed from the catwalk to the main deck at the bow.

The height of the deck cargo restricted visibility from the main wheel house, so a canvas enclosure was installed around the wheel on the flying bridge. All steering and navigation would be done from there.

A Liberty ship's crew consists of 38 officers and men and a Navy Armed Guard of one officer and about 10 men. The deck watches were broken into the 12 to 4, 4 to 8 and 8 to 12 with 2 Able Seamen and one Ordinary Seaman on each watch. My watch on the Billings was the 12 to 4, during which we would spend 2 hours on the wheel, 2 hours on lookout, with the third person on standby and alternating between stations. All deck lookouts were stood in the crows nest, with rare exceptions in severe weather. DeWayne Schwanke, as bos'n., was in charge of the deck crew and reported to the chief mate. His focile (cabin) was shared with the ship's carpenter, a quiet, likable guy from California. The other Able Seaman on my watch was Jack Hughes, from North Redondo Beach, California, married and the father of a young daughter. The Ordinary Seaman was Art Crane, a nice young guy from Glendale. The three of us shared our focile on the starboard side, main deck, just forward of DeWayne's quarters. The quarters were small, with three bunks, three lockers and not much else. A porthole opened to the deck and sea.

The captain of the Billings was about 35 years old, quiet and likable. The chief mate was about 26 years old and the 2nd and 3rd mate about the same age or a little younger. I recognized the 2nd mate, Doug Houston, as being a Maritime officer on Catalina, while I was in training there. He was a Mormon, a fine officer and gentleman and the officer in charge of my watch. We became good friends on the trip. Most of the crew were good guys and dedicated to their job. We had a few odd characters and a couple of big mouth braggarts, but that could be expected on any ship. We had one black member in the Stewarts department who served as night baker. His name was Warren and, because of his color, a number of the crew ignored him. I could sense his loneliness and always made it a point to chat with him when I had the opportunity.

I was appointed as ship's delegate, with duties of extra time keeping, settling arguments or disputes and representing the crew in matters to be taken before the captain. Our regular watches totaled 56 hours per week and seamen were compensated at 90 cents per hour for those hours worked over the 56 with the exception of any time spent for ships safety or security. Able Bodied Seamen were paid $100.00 per month and, since we were carrying a cargo of explosives, we received an additional $5.00 per month. In addition, when our ship entered the war zone, we received a 100% bonus for a total of $210.00 per month. An additional bonus of $5.00 per day was added when our ship entered an area defined as the "Battle Area". I kept records of any extra hours worked, by members of the crew, which would entitle us to overtime pay of 90 cents per hour.

With all cargo loaded and secured and the booms topped, we left San Pedro for the South Pacific and the Indian Ocean. The passage through the Timor Sea, North of Australia, had been closed since the start of the war and was under control of the Japanese. This meant our voyage would take us South of Australia, through the Tasman Sea, by Tasmania, and then up through the Indian Ocean to the Hooghly River and Calcutta. We would stay a safe distance West of Sumatra , since Japan operated a submarine base from there.

We expected to pick up a convoy en route south, but that did not happen. Our orders were to travel alone, unescorted, and I wondered if our cargo of TNT influenced that decision.

The first several weeks at sea were uneventful and the weather was great. We stopped briefly at the Island of Manus, in the New Hebrides, and I checked to see if Boo, Joe or Bob were there. They were not! The main base at Espiritu Santo, next to Manus, was occupied by Navy and Air Force personnel. We had a Navy signalman on our ship, a minor league ball player who we called "Bean" and, since I wanted information from each island, I approached "Bean" and asked for his assistance. He was a great guy and agreed to obtain the information for me. From the ship, Manus appeared to have suffered a great deal either from bombardment or storm, since the palm trees that remained standing were shredded.

Several days south of the New Hebrides, we encountered a change in the weather. Early one afternoon, the sky darkened and wind increased to near gale force. I was on watch when the entire deck crew was called out for ship's safety. The port boom on the number five hatch had vibrated out from the pins where it was shackled to the cross trees on the after mast. The boom had dropped about 2/3 of the way before it was restrained by the hoisting cable. From that position, it became a giant battering ram, crashing into our port life raft with each roll of the ship. When the ship rolled to starboard, the boom swung back and then repeated the demolition. It was necessary that the boom be lassoed and secured to the port life raft, to prevent more serious damage! It took a number of attempts before we had the boom lashed securely, with damage limited to the boom and the life raft. Realizing that the pins on the other topped booms could also vibrate out, the chief mate expressed his concern but felt it was too risky to go aloft in this wind and sea. With that, DeWayne Schwanke volunteered that he a nd I would go aloft and wire the pins in! The wind was now blowing so hard that it was impossible to stand without holding onto something, and the ship was often taking waves over the deck cargo! DeWayne and I climbed to the cross trees on the after mast and he held my legs as I slid, on my stomach, out to where the booms were shackled. I wired all the pins on the remaining booms topped to the after mast. We then started forward, over the deck cargo, when I questioned our ability to reach and secure the booms topped on the main mast due to the increasing wind and storm! DeWayne said we could do it, so we raced forward and leaped over the catwalk. I was in the lead as we scurried up the ladder on the main mast. About half way up, the ship rolled hard to port and took a giant wave over the deck cargo, catching DeWayne about at the waist, nearly dragging him off the ladder into the sea! That did it! Our eyes met for only a fraction of, a second and the fear and concern was evident as we both shouted, "Let's get the hell out of here!" We lost no time, on the starboard roll, to descend the ladder and reach the safety of the superstructure!

All outside deck watches were canceled since it was impossible to go on deck without being washed overboard! Access to the wheel on the Flying Bridge was through the interior of the ship to the main bridge, then up an exposed ladder on the starboard side. We continued to steer, or attempt to steer, from the canvas enclosed wheel house on the Flying Bridge.

The storm increased, with winds registering 80 knots. We found ourselves caught in a trough and could not break out to head the ship into the sea. The waves created the appearance of giant valleys and hills. Since we were in the trough, we would be at the bottom of the "valley" and then at the top of the "hill". The list, as the ship continued to roll, was awesome! In order to remain standing, while on wheel watch, it was necessary to lock my arms into the wheel for the port roll and reverse my hold on the starboard roll! The heavy deck cargo made the vessel somewhat top heavy and was a serious concern, as we watched the clinometer (list indicator) reach the maximum safety point, time after time! With each roll, the ship would hesitate for a time, which seemed very long, then begin a heavy vibration before recovering and starting the alternate roll. The captain told us to try to break from the trough if we saw any lessening of wave action, but to be careful not to lose our rudder. For several days, each wheel watch tried, but without success. On my wheel watch, I would watch the seas closely and, when they appeared to be less than 20 feet high, would try a hard left rudder, since the sea seemed to remain off our port. As soon as the ship started to shudder, I would bring the wheel back to mid-ship to avoid the risk of rudder loss.

Someone left the watertight door open on the starboard side, since the seas were then only breaking over the port bow and side. It was a mistake! I was trying to get some sleep before my P.M. watch call, when I was awakened by seamen shouting! I swung from my bunk, dropping my feet to the deck, into about six inches of cold sea water! Jack Hughes and Art Crane were already out of our focile and I intended to be right behind them. I reached for my life jacket, which I always placed on the top our lockers. It wasn't there! I started through our focile door and down the companionway toward the mess hall and met Warren, the night baker. Warren was bringing my life jacket to me! Art Crane had left his jacket on the boat deck, when he slept there a week before, and grabbed mine by mistake. He realized his error when he reached the mess hall, since I had my personal "abandon ship" kit attached to it, but he hesitated to bring it back to me. Warren then grabbed the jacket and was sloshing through the water to my quarters! I always felt grateful to have Warren as a friend, and never forgot his concern. The initial reaction was that our Liberty ship had cracked a seam and was breaking up, as some Liberty ships had done. The problem was simple, however, since a huge wave had broken over the aft section of the ship and flooded the companionways and quarters, on the starboard side, before the watertight doors were secured. The life preservers would have served no purpose, had the ship broken up, since no one could have survived in that sea and no life boats or rafts could have been launched. They still gave some feeling of security.

The storm continued and displayed undisputed evidence of the tremendous power of nature. During my daytime wheel watch, I witnessed the strength of the wind and storm, which I could hardly believe possible! Some of the 2x6 boards, which were nailed and cabled around the enclosure for the deck cargo, were being ripped from beneath the cables and catapulted high into the air, breaking and splintering as they struck the cable shrouds, giving the appearance of huge arrows being launched by some unseen giant hand!

Since the sky never opened, no star or sun sights could be taken and our position remained unknown. It would not have helped, had we been able to determine our position, since we were unable to steer the vessel. We simply managed, for the most part, to keep the ships rudder straight. After the fourth day of the storm, the wind and sea subsided and the sky opened. All deck officers were busy with their sextants to determine our position. We learned that we had been blown over 400 miles north of our position when the storm first hit! Everyone welcomed the hot meals again and was thankful that we had weathered the storm.

I quietly thanked the Good Lord that we had come through that awesome wind and sea safely and hoped that I would not experience another such event at sea. That was not to be!

A little over a year later, in the same general area, on a new T-2 Tanker carrying 135,000 barrels of fuel, we were disabled and encountered a near duplicate of the storm experienced on the S.S. Billings. I will describe the events of that trip later.

Our inspection, after the storm, disclosed the damage, which was much less than we expected. Other than the broken boom and damaged life raft, the catwalk was washed away, along with the ladder from the top of the deck cargo to the bow. The shoring and framing around the deck cargo was ripped away or loose, but the deck cargo was still in place.

Several nights after the storm, our watch was called at usual at 11:30 P.M. to meet our 12 to 4 stand. We always met in the mess hall for coffee, before going on watch, and chatted with members of the engine crew who were also coming on watch. In addition, there usually would be several there from the 8 to 12 watch, who were on stand by. This particular night, the chatter was about the spirits of those who had been lost at sea. Seamen are a superstitious lot and like to talk about all sorts of supernatural events. Due to the continuing rough sea, the crows nest watch had been transferred to bow lookout and the Navy Armed Guard had canceled their watch in the forward gun tub. My first watch at midnight was the bow lookout and *I* didn't want to hear their chatter. When they continued, thinking that their stories would scare me, I warned them to never try to sneak up on me to scare me, since I really didn't know how I would react!

As I relieved the 8 to 12 bow watch, he commented how lonely and spooky it was up there alone that night. It was very dark and the wind was still quite strong. I agreed that it was both spooky and lonely up there and told him that I would stand on top of the deck cargo for my lookout and not climb down to the bow. About 1/2 hour into my watch, the bow phone rang and, thinking it was the mate on the bridge, I scurried down the cargo to the phone on the bow, picked it up and reported, "Bow lookout!" There was silence and I repeated my station. With that, an evil laugh cackled over the phone and I slammed the phone down. I was wearing my pea coat over a turtle neck sweater and, now that I was on the bow, protected from the wind, I took the pea coat off, draped it over the starboard bits, and slipped back against the anchor winch, under the gun tub. After a few minutes, I heard a scraping, shuffling noise which seemed to be coming from the starboard side of the deck cargo! I pressed closely against the winch and listened! The deck cargo was stacked flush against the gunwale on both sides of the ship, and yet, I distinctly heard shuffling along the gunwale! The hair on my neck bristled and the adrenalin started to flow! If someone was approaching the bow, they had to be scooting along on the gunwale, holding onto deck cargo cables. It seemed insane and nearly impossible! Suddenly, I saw a form ease from the gunwale to the deck on the bow and was now creeping toward my pea coat, which I had draped over the bits. He thought the coat was me! I always carried a sheath knife, for line splicing or severing a line, if necessary, and kept the blade razor sharp. I unsheathed my knife and slid out behind the creeping form. When he was about 4 feet behind my coat, I lunged forward, threw my left arm around his chest and brought the knife edge up against his throat as I shouted, "Die, you son-of-a-bitch!" He let out a blood curdling scream and yelled, "It's me Rube, Fiefield, don't do it! It's me, Fiefield!" I was really angry and held him there saying, "You son-of-a-bitch, I should cut your throat!" He started to whimper as I heard other voices coming from on top the deck cargo. About four guys were involved in their scare attempt, and all were yelling that it was Tom Fiefield. They now recognized the error of their foolish stunt and were trying to apologize, asking what they could do to make amends! I had two of them spend the remaining part of my bow watch with me, to deprive them of some sleep! Tom Fiefield came from a wealthy family in Brawley, California, was not very fond of work, but was basically a nice guy, just spoiled from having life too easy! No one ever attempted any scare tactics with me or anyone else after that event. Actually, all relief watches, crows nest or bow, would call out their name to me before approaching my night watches. I preferred it that way!

Our deck engineer was a little Irishman, whom we simply called, "Deck". He liked to boast about nearly everything and most of the crew often went out of their way to avoid him. "Deck" had brought along a little black Scotch terrier from Long Beach. The dog was a favorite with everyone and would alternate between crew quarters, often sleeping at the foot of my bunk. Several days out of Melbourne, Australia, "Blackie", the terrier, became quite ill and Deck took her to a vet as soon as we docked. We learned that surgery was necessary since Blackie had been licking fish oil from the deck and had ingested a quantity of rust. We applied fish oil to the metal decks to loosen rust particles before chipping and painting. When Deck returned with his dog and told us what the vet had charged, we were surprised that he would pay that much to save his dog, and told him so. He expounded, "Why, that dog means more to me than life itself, I would do anything for that dog!" We proceeded to tease and bait him over his professed devotion. "What if you had to abandon ship, Deck?" "I wouldn't leave this ship without my dog!" he went on and on. He said that he would share his water and food rations in a life boat, if necessary, to save his little dog. We told Deck that we admired his great devotion but would question same under severe conditions. Not too many weeks later we learned how sincere and devoted Deck really was and will describe his devotion later.

The very first priority upon reaching port was to inquire about mail for our ship. Mail was so very important and everyone was anxious to hear from home and loved ones. I was always anxious to hear if Boo, Joe, Bob and Ferd were OK and hope for some hint as to where they were. I also expected to hear from Jane and looked forward to her letters. I missed her very much! We were all disappointed when we learned the sad news - "No mail for the Billings, it probably has been sent to your next port of call." That meant Calcutta, more than a month away! Little did we think, at that time, the "No mail" answer would become familiar to us!

Melbourne was a real surprise, appearing as though the clock were turned back 50 years! Horse drawn carriages were common and a type of stage coach was used to convey passenger from the train terminal to a destination of some distance. We learned that it would take several days to repair our ship and replenish our supplies. Unfortunately, the meat portion of our supplies would be mutton and domestic rabbit, a diet that we tired of rather quickly. To this day, DeWayne will not eat domestic rabbit and I doubt if he will eat mutton. With the time in port, we had the chance to explore the city and become familiar with their customs. Most of our crew agreed that we should celebrate our safe arrival and meet at one of the best hotels in Melbourne, where they had a live orchestra, dining and dancing. All was going well at the celebration until everyone had a bit too much to drink, when a late arrival from our deck crew entered the club. This was Charlie Conway, a tall, outgoing strange character who operated under the theory that, since he spent a certain amount of money each week for pleasure when he was ashore, he would add the number of weeks at sea and spend the cumulative amount in the few days in port. This made him popular with girls, waiters and orchestra leaders! We called him "Big Time Charlie". The orchestra whipped out a fanfare and Charlie entered the room, bowing and scraping! He was wearing something like a zoot suit and looked rather strange with the butch haircut I had given him just before we reached port. Apparently the Aussie girls thought he was some sort of celebrity and several left an adjoining table and came to our table to chat. Their Australian army dates didn't appreciate this and harsh words came our way. When we returned harsh words, the air thickened and a big fight developed. It didn't last very long, since the local police and the management made very strong suggestions that we depart the premises! We did!

Nearly everything was rationed in Australia and gasoline was nearly nonexistent. The taxi cabs in Melbourne were powered by a charcoal burner mounted on the rear of the vehicle. Periodically, the driver would have to stop and stoke up the fire or add more charcoal. I don't know how this worked but I assumed that the burner created some gas to power the cab. The power was limited, however, and we often had to get out and push on uphill grades.

Tony, Wayne Ulberg's brother in law, and I hit a few of the pubs on our last night in Melbourne and were sampling a brew called "Melbourne Bitter", a strong beer. At one of the pubs we were approached by several loud mouthed, bragging Australians, who said they operated some tug boats in the harbor. Tony introduced himself and then introduced me as the "Chief Mate" on the Billings. I went along with the masquerade. As they bragged about their skills, they also complained about the shortages and supply problems with which they had to contend. Tony commented that we had no problems on our ship and, as a matter of fact, actually had a surplus of nearly every supply. I went along with that and when they mentioned that they couldn't get mooring lines, I told them that we had thrown some slightly used mooring lines overboard just before reaching port since we thought we may need the space. It was ridiculous but they believed me. With that, one wanted to buy some surplus lines but I refused. He was getting rather obnoxious and insisted that I sell some to him. He continued to insist so I sold him some for 15 pounds. The big mouth paid me and I gave him a receipt. It was a nasty thing to do, but the Melbourne Bitter beer we had consumed, together with his arrogant insistence, seemed like a great thing to do at the time! Tony and I decided to leave that pub, in search of some lighter beverage.

Several girls, at the pub, suggested that we accompany them to a place noted for their good wine. We did, and it turned out to be a wild goose chase. The wine supplier apparently was a relative of one of the girls and operated his wine business out of his basement. We sampled his wine, paid him and left. When we realized that we were far removed from where we started and didn't really know where we were, and the hour was very late, we were concerned about getting back in time for sailing! We caught a funny looking trolley car, which held only about 6 people, and rode to the end of his line. A police car took us from there to the train station, but we still had about 5 miles to go to the ship. There were no more trains that night, since the all stopped running at midnight, along with the taxi cabs! A stage coach driver was dozing in his stage across from the station and we persuaded him to take us to the ship. We offered him his regular fare plus a tip of 5 pounds (about $16.50) if he could get us there by 5:00 A.M. He snapped his whip over the horses and we were off at a fast pace. We bounced over cobblestones for the first several miles and then the horses slowed to nearly a walk. Tony liked the walk since he was getting awfully sick and he said his head really hurt. I was not feeling very well either but was more concerned that we would miss our ship, so I reminded the driver of his tip. He brought out his whip and the horses broke into a trot. As we rounded the last bend, the Billings was still there, a most welcome sight!

I expected to see only the gangway watch, since it was almost 5:00 A.M., but it appeared that the entire Navy Armed Guard was out lining the rails of the ship. When they saw us, they bombarded us with some nasty names! A number of them were suggesting that I was infected with lice and that my father neglected to marry my mother! I was appalled at their outburst and couldn't understand their hostile attitude! One then told us that early in the evening, a group of Australian men came to the ship to pick up some mooring lines and showed a receipt signed by "Chief Mate" Ray Ruby. When the ship's officers refused, they became rather hostile and threatened force to get the lines. As a result, all shore leaves were canceled and the Armed Guard required to stand guard duty through the entire night. Many "last night in port" dates were left stranded and a rather unkind attitude toward me prevailed! I felt badly about the Loud Mouth Aussie's 15 pounds and would have returned it, if I knew how to get it to him.

A quick change of clothes and a struggling deck crew turned to for departure. It was a great effort to take in the gangway and lines and prepare for sea. My head hurt but poor Tony was really miserable! We both decided that alcoholic beverages could be bad for our health and agreed to behave in the future!

***

We rounded the Southern tip of Australia, by Tasmania, through the Tasman Sea and headed North through the Indian Ocean. The weather warmed quickly and soon became nearly unbearable, with temperature well above 100 degrees. I had developed a work schedule under which I would arise at 7:30 A.M., have breakfast and turn to for work detail from 8:00 to 11:00. I would then eat lunch and report on watch at 12:00 until 4:00 P.M., then a work detail from 4:00 to 5:00. I would then have supper at 6:00 and hit the bunk about 8:00. My watch would then be called at 11:30 P.M. for watch duty from midnight until 4:00 A.M., then back to the bunk until 7:30 A.M. again. This made an 80 hour work week but gave me 24 hours of overtime pay. With overtime at 90 cents per hour, this came to $21.60 each week to be credited to my account and paid when the voyage was over.

The hot weather in the Indian Ocean really sapped me and I began to lose weight. My appetite disappeared and I skipped breakfast, drank tea only for lunch and supper, and only had what dessert they offered for supper. Regular use of salt tablets and a lot of water became my regular diet. By the time we reached Calcutta, I weighed 25 pounds less than when we left Melbourne.

I thought that Captain Abramson would be angry with me for the mooring line incident and fully expected to be called to his quarters. Several days passed and nothing was said! I assumed the matter was forgotten. A few days later, however, while I was on the wheel, the captain came on the bridge, walked back and forth a few times, and addressed me. "Ruby, have you been to India before?" "No sir!" I answered. "It's a strange country and beggars are everywhere," he continued, "Now, as we approach India, I want you to remember how many life boats and life rafts are on this ship. When we sail back down the Hooghly I expect to see the same number still on board, so don't sell or give away anything!" "I certainly understand, Captain, and assure you that nothing will be missing!" I replied. As I looked over to the captain, I could see a big grin on his face. I knew that he wasn't angry with me, but a few of the Armed Guard remained somewhat cool!

Our captain was warned, before leaving Melbourne, that Japanese submarines, from a base in Sumatra, were active in the Indian Ocean. Our course would take us more than 200 miles West of Sumatra, so we did not expect any problems. About 10 days out of Melbourne, I was in the crows nest when battle stations sounded. I could see that the Navy Armed Guard, in the forward gun tub, was scanning the skies off our port bow. I kept looking but couldn't see anything due to looking up in the direction of the bright sun light. It wasn't until I heard the airplane engines that I realized that an aircraft was approaching with the sun behind it. It seemed on a gentle descent, directly to our ship, much too slow for a fighter aircraft. When identified, it was one of ours, a Catalina Flying Boat, probably just curious and wanted to be recognized. After days of inactivity, any different event gets to be exciting and starts the adrenalin to flow.

Several days after the aircraft sighting, I finished my watch at 4:00 A.M. and was in my bunk fast asleep at 4:30. The ship's bells sounded and, in my half conscious mind, I counted them. Battle stations! Jack Hughes shook me and yelled, "Come on Rube, battle stations!" I pulled on my trousers, grabbed my life jacket and slipped on my shoes. As I left my focile, I noticed "Blackie", the terrier, asleep at the foot of my bunk. My battle station was in the bow gun tub, to assist as the number 2 loader for the four inch 50 cannon. As the shells came up the elevator, a seaman would grab the shell and pass it to me, and I would then pass it to the number 1 loader and step aside for the hot shell casing to be ejected to a "hot shell man", who would throw the spent casing overboard as we repeated the process. On my way to the gun tub, I saw "Deck" just forward of the superstructure, holding onto the starboard rail. He was really upset! "See it Rube, look out there, we don't have a chance!" I looked and about one point forward of the starboard beam, about 200 yards out, was a surfaced submarine. Although it was barely light, the craft was easily identified, and since they would be looking up from the surface, there could be no question that they had seen us. I never knew just how I would react to imminent danger and refused to speculate or worry about it. That morning, however, I had no fear, just a tired resignation, knowing that if they scored any hit on our vessel, the 8,800 tons of TNT would erase any sign of our ship! I think the previous weeks of scorching weather and fatigue left me with a "don't much care" attitude. "Deck" grabbed my arm and he was shaking badly, sort of whimpering, as he said, "Why don't we fire at them, they are going to sink us, why don't we fire!" I said, "Deck, just pray that we don't fire, because we'll miss him and make him mad, we have a better chance by continuing as though we didn't see him, and hope that their vessel is disabled!" I then added, "Deck, where is Blackie?" He didn't answer so I repeated my question. Deck then shouted, "Oh, the hell with Blackie, who can think of a dog at a time like this!" We never let Deck forget that morning, although I'm sure that he would have liked to. The submarine suddenly dove and we waited, for what seemed a long while, to see or hear a surface torpedo, but none ever came! The gunnery officer said it was an enemy sub since we had no submarines operating in those waters at that time. In any event, his decision not to fire was a wise one and

I respected him for that. I saw our gunners in practice at sea, and after witnessing their "skills", I felt somewhat insecure! There may still be some 55 gallon drums, painted yellow with zinc chromate, floating around in the South Pacific. Those were the drums we painted and threw over the stern for cannon practice. I watched, with increasing lack of confidence, as shell after shell exploded long, short, left and right, until the barrels bobbed out of sight!

The remaining weeks to Calcuta were uneventful except for sighting huge tree trunks and debris floating about 200 miles off the coast of Burma. There had been a very great storm in Burma, which uprooted trees and caused great floods, forcing debris far into the ocean. I wondered if this was part of the same storm which we encountered off the coast of Australia.

I noticed, as we approached the mouth of the Hooghly River, I could "smell" India, even though we were many miles from land. That country has a distinctive smell, one that I shall not forget. I noticed a somewhat similar smell, some years later, as we drove through the little town of Des Arc, Missouri, one fall night, on our way to Clearwater Lake. I guess it was the many cooking fires, mixed with the night air which created the similar smell.

The Hooghly is a muddy stream, similar to the Mississippi with the exception of the dead animal carcasses and the Hindu "Bum Boats". It is a long, tricky body of water to navigate and could not be accomplished without the aid of an experienced river pilot. Our navigational pilot was picked up about 20 miles from the mouth of the river.

As we steamed up the Hooghly, we passed a number of Hindu Bum boats rowing or paddling upstream. As we were preparing to pass one, it appeared as if the Hindus were attempting to draw close to our vessel. As we overtook them, they threw a line with a grappling hook which caught on the aft rail at the stern. They were then being pulled along upstream, making the appearance of a ski boat containing about 10 men, all of whom were grinning widely. I thought they were pretty clever and was glad that they had hooked on to ease their upstream efforts. Bob Williams, an ordinary seaman, whom I had nicknamed "Big Hank", because he reminded me of the dumb "Big Hank" who accompanied me on my first voyage, came back to the stern to watch. After a few minutes, he suddenly picked up a fire axe, and before anyone could stop him, severed the tow line, nearly capsizing their boat! I was shocked! "Why in the world did you do that, they weren't hurting anything? I asked. "I don't know", he answered. Big Hank was stupid!

We finally arrived at King George docks, our destination in Calcutta. First order of business, after docking and securing our vessel, was to check for mail for the Billings. The same answer came back, "No mail for the Billings, it will probably be at your next port of call." It wasn't!

India is a strange country, with extreme poverty and disease everywhere. Our entire crew received 27 different shots and vaccinations before leaving the states and during the voyage. Diseases which were unknown or long forgotten in our part of the world existed here and I felt so sorry for these poor people. At that time, the average wage for labor was less than several dollars (in our money) per month! Cows are considered sacred, as are monkeys, the earth and the river. Sacred cows and monkeys wander through the streets and market place, with vehicles and pedestrians giving them a wide berth.

Most transportation was by rickshaw and we employed those drivers to take us through the city. On one such trip, an extremely thin, emaciated looking driver attempted to get us to hire him. I hesitated because he didn't appear strong enough to pull my buddy and me. He insisted, so we felt sorry for him and hired him. About half way, he stumbled a few times and then fell down. We thought he was dying, so we picked him up, put him in the rickshaw and took turns pulling. A few blocks further, as I was pulling, I looked back to see the Hindu, seated next to my buddy, and he was smiling broadly, having fully recovered. I had the feeling that we had been "had" and that our driver had stumbled and fallen a few times with other customers. We continued to our destination, paid the driver, and he happily trotted away!

There were only three places, in Calcutta, where food or drink could be safely purchased. These were "Firpo's Restaurant", the King George Hotel and the Merchant Seaman's Club. We invited all our Navy Armed Guard personnel to use our Seaman's Club since prices were reasonable and no U.S.O. or Servicemen's facilities were to be found in the city. I met several young Burmese children, who were staying at the Seamen's Club. They were about 7 or 8 years old and were part of the incredible "children's march" from Rangoon, Burma, through very difficult terrain, to escape the Japanese when they captured Burma. One little boy spoke English fairly well, was very outgoing, so we hired him as a guide and "negotiator" to assist us in moving about in the city and in purchasing souvenirs. He was delighted and stayed with us the entire time we were in Calcutta, probably saving us a lot of money.

I remained on board for security watch one day, as DeWayne Schwanke and several others went into the city. When DeWayne returned, he displayed a bright anchor tattoo on his right forearm. He said, since we were good buddies, and agreed to do everything together I should also get a tattoo! It was a stupid idea but, at the time, it sounded like a good plan! DeWayne and I went into the city the next day and visited the back alley Hindu tattoo artist. I selected an eagle, carrying an anchor with two American flags. An eagle carrying an anchor doesn't make any sense but, at the time, I thought it looked nice. DeWayne burned the tattoo needle with a match and the Hindu proceeded to punch thousands of holes in my arm! The tattoo is very faded now but shall always remain with me as my "badge of ignorance!"

***

One day, a ship mate and I were in town and wanted to find a safe place to buy some ice cream. None was available at any of the three approved spots. As we were walking down the street, we saw a man coming toward us, dressed in sun tans, and we assumed that he was a part of the 20th Bomber Command, since some of their members often came into Calcutta on a pass or short leave. We asked him about ice cream. He said he would take us to a shop where it was safe to eat the ice

Joe – U.S. Army – Service in Southwest Pacific.

Ferd – U.S. Army – Service in European theatre.

Leonard (Boo) – U.S. Army - Service in Southwest Pacific.

Bob – U.S. Marines - Service in Southwest Pacific.

Ray – U.S. Merchant Marine – Service in Pacific, Atlantic and
Indian Oceans.

Tom – U.S. Army – Service stateside.

10,000-TON TANKER ADRIFT 17 HOURS

A U.S. ship which was adrift for 17 hours with disabled engines during a voyage from America reached Sydney yesterday under her own power.

She is the tanker Whittier Hills (10,000 tons).

Whittier Hills was adrift in a heavy sea while her crew repaired her engines.

Just before the engines were restarted, the ship drifted in a four-knot current to within 10 miles of a reef.

The crew said yesterday that the ship's engines gave trouble from the time she left San Pedro (California), and broke down last Tuesday, 300 miles east of Cape Moreton (Queensland).

The breakdown was caused by condensor tubes leaking saltwater into the boiler system, and the salt affecting the automatic equipment.

Inspection plates had to be removed from the main condensors, leaking tubes plugged, and the evaporator cleaned out.

No Permanent Damage

The chief engineer (Mr. Buckley) and first engineer, who had already spent nearly all their time in the engine-room, were helped in repair work by the engine-room staff and volunteers from the deck.

Mr. Buckley, a former lieutenant-colonel in the U.S. Army Engineers, was nearly electrocuted while working on a jammed turbine governor.

The breakdown did no permanent damage to the engines, and only minor repairs are now necessary.

Whittier Hills will discharge her cargo of petrol and kerosene, and return to America. oh yeah!

Tanker Adrift.—With her engines disabled the U.S. tanker Whittier Hills is drifting in heavy seas 300 miles east of Brisbane. (p. 1)

76-Hour Fight To Save Drifting Tanker

When the 10,000-ton tanker Whittier Hills arrived in Sydney yesterday the engineer officers and the engine-room crew showed signs of the strain of 76 hours almost continuous work without sleep.

The tanker's boilers "salted-up" at 8.30 a.m. on Tuesday and the vessel drifted helplessly about 300 miles off Brisbane.

It was in a dangerous situation, drifting towards Middleton Reef.

The five engineer officers, the engine-room crew of 12, and the deck crew of eight began work immediately, and by 1.55 a.m. on Wednesday one boiler had been freed of salt. The tanker was able to resume its voyage at half-speed—six knots.

Twelve hours later the second boiler was clean and the tanker was able to steam at full-speed for Sydney.

None of the engineers had any sleep from 8.30 a.m. on Tuesday until 1 p.m. to-day," said the chief engineer, Commander John R. Buckley. "I have never seen men work so hard. In 12 hours they did as much work as would normally be done in two weeks."

Commander Buckley said that he would supervise the retubing of the condens. and other repairs himself. No damage had been done to the engines themselves.

The Whittier Hills, commanded by Captain J. W. Mahoney, is owned by the U.S. War Shipping Administration and operated by Los Angeles Tankers Incorp. Its Sydney agents are the Vacuum Oil Co. Pty., Ltd.

It brought 2,400,000 gallons of petrol and 1,600,000 gallons of power kerosene from San Pedro, in California. Half is for Sydney and the rest for Newcastle and Brisbane.

RAYMOND LEO RUBY

To you who answered the call of your country and served in its Merchant Marine to bring about the total defeat of the enemy, I extend the heartfelt thanks of the Nation. You undertook a most severe task—one which called for courage and fortitude. Because you demonstrated the resourcefulness and calm judgment necessary to carry out that task, we now look to you for leadership and example in further serving our country in peace.

Harry Truman

THE WHITE HOUSE

U.S. Department
of Transportation

**Maritime
Administration**

Administrator

400 Seventh Street S.W.
Washington, D.C. 20590

Dear Merchant Marine Veteran:

Pursuant to the January 19, 1988, official conferment of veteran status on members of the American Merchant Marine who served aboard oceangoing merchant ships on World War II, I am pleased to provide you with your wartime Certificate of Service. Certainly, this long overdue recognition was well-earned. The officers and crews played a key role in transporting the troops and war material that enabled United States and Allied Forces to turn the tide of victory against the Axis powers.

In providing this vital wartime service, the American Merchant Marine paid a heavy toll. President Ronald Reagan acknowledged this cost recently, in his 1988 National Maritime Day Proclamation, when he stated, "The importance of the merchant marine to our national defense was never more clear than in World War II when, at a cost of more than 6,000 lives and with a loss of 733 ships, the American merchant marine never faltered in delivering cargo for our Armed Forces throughout the world." U.S merchant seamen died as a result of enemy attacks at a rate that proportionately exceeded all branches of our armed services, with the single exception of the United States Marine Corps. Untold thousands of additional seafarers were wounded or injured in these attacks, and nearly 600 were made prisoners of war.

We in the Department of Transportation and the Maritime Administration staunchly supported the efforts to provide veteran status for World War II seafarers.

The Honorable Discharge and Form DD 214, which you have received from the U.S. Coast Guard or the Department of the Army, entitle you to certain benefits administered by the Veterans' Administration. You should contact your nearest Veterans' Administration office to determine the benefits available to you.

Sincerely,

JOHN GAUGHAN
Maritime Administrator

Enclosure

United States Merchant Marine

Certificate of Service

This is to certify that

RAYMOND LEO RUBY

is a

U.S. Merchant Marine Veteran

having served aboard oceangoing merchant ships in service to the
United States during World War II.

MARITIME ADMINISTRATOR

cream which they sold. He had an accent, but we didn't ask him about his unit. When we reached the shop, we asked him to join us for the ice cream and he accepted. He then told us that he was an Italian prisoner of war, having been captured on the very first day that the Axis powers and England declared war. He was on submarine duty and was submerged when his sub was destroyed. He didn't know how he survived or if any other members of his crew made it. He had been a prisoner so long that they now had given a number of the prisoners "Trustee" status, and they could come and go as they pleased, reporting back to their quarters at a set time each day. He was an intelligent and interesting gentleman and we enjoyed talking to him. He asked if we would like to see his prison barracks and we said we would. He took us to their quarters and I was surprised to see what they had created with their ingenuity. The barracks were spotless and all the contents had been made by them. Their bunks, chairs and tables were all hand made from native wood and woven barks. I was impressed. When our visit ended, he insisted that we take some of their home made "raisin jack" (raisin wine) back to the ship with us. Since the incident in Melbourne, I wasn't interested in any alcoholic drink but didn't want to hurt his feelings. He placed several large bottles in a burlap sack and we returned to the ship. I went aboard first and lowered a line off the bow to my ship mate, he tied the line to the sack of wine and I hoisted it aboard. The other crew members said the wine was good and appreciated the gift.

Disease and famine resulted in many deaths daily in India. Hindus pulling a cart would travel the streets each morning, collect the dead bodies and take them to one of the "Burning Ghats" in the city. The Hindu religion calls for burning the dead and the "Ghats" were enclosures for this purpose, open to the sky, where the dead were placed on a hand made frame and woven bier, covered with brush and sticks and burned. We visited the Nimtahla Burning Ghats to witness the ceremony and the burning. It was a little too much! Before igniting the fire, the ceremony consisted of rubbing oil on the head of the deceased, painting the soles of his feet and mixing his last meal. This meal was a banana and rice, all squashed together and then stuffed in his mouth. Green flies were everywhere! When the body started to burn, the odor got to us and we retreated a distance. The unburned bones and remains were finally tossed into the "Sacred Hooghly" river to float downstream to the ocean. Just downstream from the Ghats maiden girls swam, allegedly, to capture the strength and spirit of the deceased. India is a strange country with strange customs and I will never forget the people affected by "Yaws" or "Elephantitis"! I made a pledge to never complain about any of my circumstances and to help the poverty stricken when ever I could.

Native crews were employed to help discharge our cargo of TNT and, since labor was so cheap, were also employed to paint the ship while we were in port. They hung from poorly made scaffolds and swings as they painted the bulkheads and masts. Didn't look very safe to me but they completed the painting, doing a fairly good job. I continued to be appalled at the lack of sanitary facilities and the disease everywhere! Instead of a latrine, for workers on board the ship, the Hindus carried a little bucket, to which they attached a long string. I saw them urinate or defecate into this bucket, then lower it over the offshore side of the ship, splash it up and down in the water several times to wash out the contents, then draw a full bucket of water up to them and take a drink from that same can! This, together with seeing them chewing their beetle nut, which made them appear to have a mouth full of blood, gave me a sick feeling and I looked forward to our departure from this country.

When all of the TNT was discharged we started to take on a new cargo. Some of the 20th Bomber Command was now being transferred to the Marianas, where they would pilot the newer B-29s for direct bombing of Japan. We learned that our cargo would be 8000 one ton demolition bombs and detonators to be delivered to Tinian, in the Marianas. The loading of these heavy bombs, one at a time, was a slow process. One native had his foot crushed as he was assisting in the loading. All natives were without shoes, and I'm sure the pain of that mangled foot was excruciating! The bombs were loaded in a row from port to starboard, and when one completed, was covered with a layer of board dunnage for the next rows. Each bomb was wedged to avoid shifting or rolling.

The loading was finally completed and we were scheduled to sail. Several days before sailing, I was in town and was surprised to meet a former ship mate from the S.S. Fort Stevenson. He was now on a C-2 Cargo ship, a newer much faster vessel than the Liberty, and he told me that they were also taking a cargo of bombs to the Marianas. He also told me that their route to the Marianas was going to be through the Northern pass and not as they had come, around the Southern tip of Australia. His ship would be the first to use that route since the beginning of the war. Our ship was the second!

Upon leaving King George docks in Calcutta, we accidentally struck several Hindu Bum boats with our propeller (the ship's screw), doing some minor damage to our screw and considerable damage to the Bum boats! The damage to the screw would later prevent our ship from returning to the

South Pacific from Pearl Harbor. I felt sorry for the Hindus as they were thrown from their wrecked boats. We were unable to stop and continued out of the harbor and downstream.

We sailed several hours before the C-2 but they passed us going downstream. My old ship mate was on the wheel of the C-2 and I was on the wheel of the Billings when they passed. He yelled and waved to me and I did the same in return. The British river pilot reprimanded me for being momentarily distracted from the wheel. He, like most British officers I had seen, was an arrogant chap, and I added him to those whom I did not like!

The pilot boat came alongside, after we cleared the mouth of the river, and after we dropped the pilot, we started south to our next port of call. We sailed in the Western part of the Bay of Bengal and stopped at Colombo, Ceylon (now Sri Lanka). No mail here for the Billings either!

I don't know what happened in Colombo, either from the war or from a storm, but a great number of sunken ships were scattered throughout the harbor. We had a short stay and shore leave in Colombo, where good values in ivory and precious stones could be found. Jack Hughes bought a beautiful star sapphire for $27.00 and Tom Fiefield bought a fantastic model of a sailing ship, carved out of ivory and ebony. He paid $200.00 for it, an incredible price to pay for a piece of art!

Several days out of Ceylon, in the Indian Ocean, we encountered a moderate storm, causing the ship to roll. A thunderous noise started coming from the #3 hold, sounding like a giant battering ram against the hull of the ship! The entire deck crew was called out for "ship's safety" and we removed the battens and cover from the hatch, went into the hold and started chopping through the dunnage. One row of bombs, on the second layer, had not been wedged and the entire row would roll to port and then to starboard with each roll of the ship. This created about a 30 ton battering ram against the hull. The Liberty could withstand very little of that! We worked at chopping and wedging for several hours before the row was secure.

Our route past Sumatra and Java was without problems and we entered the Timor Sea enroute to Darwin, Australia. I was on the wheel as we approached Darwin, and picked up a navigational pilot, who would navigate us through the tricky straits East of Darwin. I noticed that the small pilot boat was heavily armed with anti-aircraft equipment and asked Doug Houston, the 2nd Mate, to question the pilot when he came aboard. It seemed that enemy aircraft had routinely attacked the City of Darwin, and all women and children had been evacuated from there long before. The pilot said that the raids were down to only one or two a week and he was confident that the Japanese were suffering great losses of both men and equipment in the South Pacific.

We left Darwin and sailed East through the Arafura Sea, enroute to Port Moresby, New, Guinea. The Arafura Sea was the most unusual body of water I had ever seen. Very small islands were numerous with some being no larger than a small house. In addition, some submerged islands or reefs could be seen beneath the clear water. I reported one such submerged mass while I was on lookout in the crows nest. It appeared nearly dead ahead, slightly to the port of our bow, and I feared we would strike it, since it was impossible to maneuver the vessel so quickly following my warning! We passed safely over the structure, only yards off our port side. I guess the submerged island or reef was much deeper than it appeared since the water was so crystal clear and deceiving. Schools of fish were plentiful and acres of silvery schools would glisten in the sunlight. I learned later that this area was most productive for fish of many species, also was considered the most shark infested waters.

***

I was on the wheel when we approached Port Moresby, New Guinea. The mast of a sunken ship was visible in the harbor and the captain told me to use the mast as my landmark, and steer directly toward it though the opening into the harbor. Doug Houston pointed to a huge "rip tide" outside the entrance and said that I would have to allow for that as we reached it. I acknowledged and watched it carefully as we approached. The mate didn't say which direction the rip tide was running but it appeared evident to me that it was running strong to port. Just before reaching the current, I put one full right rudder on the wheel, then a hard right just as we hit the tide. I felt it would take this much to compensate for the strong left current. I was horrified, as we hit and the ship started a fast turn to the right! The tide was running the opposite direction, to starboard! The captain had his glasses on the mast of the sunken ship, and was surprised when we started a long right turn! I explained the error and, after completing the long right circle, successfully entered the harbor and dropped anchor.

Our signalman got the message of "No mail for the Billings". I then had him signal for information on Boo's unit of Combat Engineers. He learned that they had been there but were there no longer. When the war ended and Boo returned home, we learned that he had been injured at Port Moresby during an air raid and was awarded the Purple Heart. Boo operated a D-8 Caterpillar and was responsible for keeping the runways open by filling bomb craters and clearing wrecked aircraft. It was during a raid when Boo, in his jeep on his way to the D-8, hit a bomb crater and was injured.

No one was allowed ashore at Port Moresby and, after a very short stay, we continued toward the Marianas. We reached the island of Guam and all were elated when Bean received the answer to his mail inquiry, "Yes, there was mail for the Billings!" We launched a lifeboat and sent three men from the armed guard with several sacks to pick up our mail. When they left for shore, I asked Bean to signal and obtain information about Bob's marine division. The answer received was that only wounded Marines were on the island and the balance of his division were either at Saipan or in Okinawa. I had Bean check the wounded and was relieved to learn that none of Bob's company was among them!

Doug Houston had offered to bet me that he would receive more mail from his wife than I would from Jane. I was confident that I would receive a lot of mail from Jane and also from Mom, and eagerly took the bet! The Navy Armed Guard finally returned with but one sack partially filled with mail! We all stood around the #4 hatch for the mail distribution with the tension and excitement evident. My name was finally called! I received but one letter and it was from Mom! I was anxious to hear from Jane but also very anxious to learn if all my brothers were OK. I clutched Mom's letter and took it to my focile, sat on my bunk and opened the envelope with shaking hands. It was the first mail we had received in nearly seven months. I couldn't believe it when I reached for the letter in the envelope, there wasn't a letter there! I turned the envelope over, peering inside again and again, as I felt a heavy lump in my throat! Jack Hughes was sitting on his bunk, reading a letter from his wife. When he finished, he looked up and asked, "Was your letter from your Mom, Rube?" I said that it was. "Well, how are your brothers, what did your Mom have to say?" he asked. "She didn't say anything, Jack!" and I handed him the envelope. I know Jack felt nearly as bad as I about my empty envelope! It was not until I returned home on leave, that I learned from Mom how the empty envelope happened to be mailed. Mom wrote each of us, including Pop, each week and it was a small wonder that more mailing mishaps did not occur. I don't know how she kept up with all the work and the worry of 5 sons overseas and Pop out of state working. I'm sure that Mom's prayers were instrumental in all of us returning home safely! Tom joined the Air Force after the war, so all six of Pop and Mom's sons served in the service of our country.

Since I had received no letters from Jane, I started up to the 2nd Mate's quarters to pay him on our bet. I met him in the companionway on his way down to my focile. He had the money in his hand saying, "Here, Ruby, I only got one letter from my wife!" I pushed his money back to him and handed him mine, "That's one more than I got from Jane!" We both just shook our heads and agreed, "Just wait until you see all the mail we'll get at our next port!"

It was only about 100 miles from Guam to Tinian and we anchored in the harbor at Tinian when we arrived. They had but one facility to discharge heavy cargo and it was in use when we arrived. We would have to await our turn.

We finally received a lot of mail at Tinian and the news I received was all good. Mom had heard from Boo, Joe, Ferd and Bob and all were OK. Ferd was now in the European theatre, just in time for the Battle of the Bulge, and would be part of the final action there. Boo, Joe and Bob were somewhere in the South Pacific, and I felt certain that Bob was in the Marianas. I had a number of letters from Jane, which I read over and over, as she filled me in on all the happenings in Jennings. Pop had taken the job in Kingsport, Tennessee and would eventually complete his out of state work in Pasco, Washington. I even got a letter from Pop, one which I especially treasured. I knew it was an effort for Pop to write and, in reading his letter I could almost see and hear him talking!

***

After the war, Tom told of an incident which occurred during a period when Pop was home on the farm. Pop was hoeing in a small field, at the base of our hill, when two well dressed young men came down our lane. They were handing out religious literature and selling bibles. After a brief conversation, Pop asked them why they were not in service. They said they were "Jehovah's Witnesses" and refused to serve since it violated their religious beliefs. They said if everyone refused to fight, we would have no wars. They encountered the wrong man! Pop called them some rather colorful and descriptive names, including some of his favorite "sons-a bitches" suggesting that their livers were a bright yellow and belonged to chickens. He wielded his hoe, as he told them to never return! They never did!

***

I went ashore at the first opportunity and checked on Bob's unit. They were not on Tinian but they wouldn't tell me where they were. I now felt certain that Bob was on Saipan and I would somehow find a way to get there! I next found a military dentist to pull two teeth which had been giving me a lot of trouble for several weeks. The dentist wouldn't pull them since he said he could save them! He pried and scraped and finally placed a hard temporary filling in each. They continued to ache for several more weeks but he was correct, he saved them and I still have them.

We counted the B-29s as they took off from Tinian each

evening and counted them as they returned in the morning. Sometimes a few stragglers would return late and we feared that they had been lost in the raid. We were always relieved when the last one approached. The runway on Tinian ended at the edge of a cliff and the heavily loaded B-29s would often disappear for a few moments, after they left the runway, drop toward the water, and finally recover to proceed on their mission. It was as awesome sight.

Air raid sirens sounded one night and we watched the anti aircraft tracers in the night sky. The 20 MM guns on our ship and the other ship in the harbor, reminded me of Roman candles on the fourth of July, but left a feeling of insecurity. I heard an aircraft but saw nothing. They said it probably was an observation plane, one of which came over quite often.

The air base on Tinian had several B-29s in a large fenced area which was off limits to everyone except a select group of personnel. We asked about the tight security around these planes, and were told that these B-29s were to deliver a very large special bomb on Japan. I envisioned a bomb several times larger than the one ton demolition bombs we delivered. Little could we have known that the enclosure protected the expected "Enola Gay" and the back up aircraft which would deliver the first atomic bombs to Hiroshima and then Nagasaki, Japan!

I continued to check on some method to get to Saipan but had not learned of a possibility until later. In the meanwhile, we launched our lifeboat with the inboard engine and used it for a means to reach a Victory ship, which had just arrived and was also at anchor. We offered to trade some of our domestic rabbit meat for some potatoes and onions. The chief mate, DeWayne and I made the trip, returning with our boat loaded nearly to the gunwales. I don't think we could have carried another sack of onions or potatoes on that boat! Since we had

the boat in the water , DeWayne and I wanted to do some
sailing and exploring in our off time. We needed a larger keel
on the life boat, so we got the carpenter to prepare a plywood
keel, which we then fastened to the lifeboat with short braces
over the existing keel and rigged two guy wires on each
side to hold it in place. In order to position the keel, it was
necessary to dive beneath the lifeboat and hold it in place while
DeWayne fastened the guy wires. I enjoyed the crystal clear
salt water and had fun assisting in the modification. When
all was completed, we were ready to test the results. The chief
mate, 2nd Mate Doug, DeWayne and I shoved off. I was the
only one wearing a shirt and long trousers, since I didn't want
the possibility of a sun burn. The others were clad only in their
swim suits. All went well, as we raised the sail and tacked
between the buoys, out of the harbor. We planned to sail to
the far end of the island to see some caves, where Japanese
soldiers were reported to be hiding. About 2/3 of the way, the
wind died and we drifted for a while. As the afternoon wore
on and the sun became hotter, we tried to start the inboard,
without success. We finally decided to break out the oars and
attempt to row back, since we were now several miles from the
harbor. Four oars just wouldn't do it against, what appeared to
be a strong tide running from the island! We tried the engine
over and over but couldn't even get it to sputter. The afternoon
passed into evening and we began to have some concern for the
direction of our drift! A small island, within sight of Tinian,
was still occupied by the Japanese, and that is the direction
we were drifting! Since the island was small and probably few
Japanese military were occupying it, our military felt it was
not worth the cost to capture it, so the Navy had a Destroyer
Escort patrol around the island on a 24 hour basis. I don't
know how many Japanese were on this island, but we could see

their cooking fires at night, and if we continued our drifting course, I feared we may find out, first hand, how many were there! I began to feel somewhat insecure! It was dusk when our chief mate took the flashlight and flashed a signal toward the D.E. and the island of Tinian. I don't know who picked up the signal, but we soon saw the wake of a fast moving Navy Launch coming in our direction. They came alongside and didn't seem very pleased. We threw them our painter line and asked them to take it easy on the way in. We had already dropped the mast. Our request to "take it easy" was completely ignored and they left with full throttle! We yelled for them to slow down but they just laughed and kept full throttle! Suddenly one guy wire broke and the other three quickly followed, as we lost our keel! The rudder then bounced out of its slot and we lost it! Our boat was skimming like a giant saucer and, without steerage, we would surely capsize. All four of us were lying flat in the boat, trying to keep it upright. DeWayne and the chief mate then slipped an oar back to the stern, secured it and then maintained some degree of steerage. As we neared the buoys, marking the entrance to the harbor, the launch released our tow line and sped away. I thought surely we would collide with one of the buoys, but we luckily sped past it. Our captain was standing on the bridge as we pulled alongside the Billings. He didn't seem too pleased! DeWayne and the two deck officers had severe sunburn and were miserable for quite some time. My shirt and trousers saved me from the same. This incident ended our sailing efforts.

***

One of our Navy Armed Guard learned that a landing craft left Tinian for Saipan each day and a pass could be obtained from the Red Cross hut, which would allow one to board the craft for the trip. I went to get a pass but when the Red Cross representative learned that I was a Merchant Marine, he refused to issue me one, since I was not a member of the military! I tried to persuade him but he became indignant and told me that he SHOULDN'T EVEN BE WASTING HIS TIME TALKING TO ME! That did it! I was angry and tired of continually being treated this way. I answered the government's call for this service and had done everything asked and required of me, but was treated as an outcast in many areas. It would be 44 years before the U.S. Congress passed legislation which recognized the Merchant Marine who served in the war zone between December 7, 1941 and the surrender of Japan in August, 1945, and were entitled to Veteran Status. I finally received my Military discharge in 1989! I went back to my ship and stewed about the Red Cross and the entire matter! I then decided that I was going to Saipan to see Bob, and had developed a plan to do so!

I approached Virg VonderHaar, a Navy Armed Guard on our ship. Virg was from St. Louis and we were good friends. I asked Virg if I could borrow one of his unmarked shirts, dungarees and white uniform caps, and told him what I wanted to do. He gave me a set of his unmarked work uniforms but told me that I was nuts to try it! I donned the clothes, went ashore and waited outside the Red Cross hut for change of their shift. When a new person went in, and the one I had originally spoken to left, I entered the hut. I identified myself, using my correct name, but told him that I was member of the Armed Guard on the S.S. Billings, and wanted to go to Saipan to contact my brother. He took my name and serial number (I gave him my "z" number since we were not issued serial numbers) and he issued their pass, which had to have the approval of the Navy Officer on board the

Billings! On my way back to the ship, I pondered over how I could get the Officer's approval without him knowing how I represented myself. I decided on flattery! On board, I changed back into my regular clothes and went to see the Navy C.O. I told him that I had been to the Red Cross and they would OK my trip to Saipan, if he would give his approval and issue a pass. I then told him how I realized what a responsible position he occupied on our ship and how much I respected and admired his sound judgment. I stressed how important it was for me to see my brother and would greatly appreciate his help. He said "Ruby, I'm glad that you recognize the awesome importance of my position, I feel a keen responsibility for all of the men on board this vessel, but I also understand your feelings in wanting to visit your brother. I know that you will be careful, so I will approve!" He then typed out a pass but placed "Merchant Marine" after my name. I still have the pass. I then needed permission from our captain to leave for several days, and found him on the bridge. I told him what I wanted to do. He paced back and forth several times and then said, "Dammit, Ruby, I can't give you permission to leave this ship and go to another island!" I told him how important this was to me and asked him to reconsider. He said "No, I cannot give you that permission!" Then, as he turned away, he added, "But I won't look for you if you're gone!" That was all I needed. I thanked him and then asked how long we would be at Tinian. He said that he didn't know, that we may be there for a month or may get orders to sail the next day! He reminded me of the penalties for missing a ship in the islands. All of the pay I earned for the many past months would be forfeited and I would be placed under the jurisdiction of the U.S. Army. I said that I understood and thanked him again.

Early the next morning, I donned Virg VonderHaar's

navy togs and waited at the landing craft. A line of about 20 men were boarding and I joined them. One sailor checked all passes as we boarded. I feared that he would see the "Merchant Marine" typed on my pass and challenge me, so I held my thumb over "Merchant Marine". He pulled my arm around, looked at the pass for a moment and let me climb aboard.

It is a short run from Tinian to Tanapaga Harbor on Saipan, and it didn't take long for us to reach there. As we docked, I realized that Bob may not even be on the island and I may have a real problem! I asked directions to the Chaplain's hut and found it with a note pinned to the door, "Gone to Guam, be back in several days.." I came back to the dock and saw a black navy man working in a small office. I greeted him, told him who I was looking for, asked if he could help me, and furnished Bob's company number. He agreed to check for me and confirmed that Bob's outfit was on the North end of the island. He made a phone call, told me to wait, and turned shortly telling me that Bob was on the phone! The island telephone connections were not very good with transmission often breaking up. When Bob was trying to give me directions, his voice kept fading, and I couldn't understand much of what was being said, I was so excited however, knowing that he was on the island, I knew I would find him! I told Bob that I would be there shortly and hung up. I started walking north! The hills to the North looked a long way off. About ½ mile down the road, a jeep pulled alongside and an officer said, "Hop in sailor. The officer was a Lutheran Chaplain from another part of the island. I told him where I was going and he said that he knew exactly where that unit was camped. After a wild, fast ride in his jeep, he stopped at a path and pointed the direction to Bob's camp. I started down the narrow path wondering why there wasn't a road or gate. I crossed a little draw and saw hundreds of tents on the next hillside. I picked the first row of tents, marked with a hand printed sign, "Easy Street". I stopped at the first tent, picked up the flap and sway that no one was there. There were four Marines in the second tent and they appeared startled as I lifted the flap. I told them who I was looking for. They said, "His tent is the next one up, but he's not there, he is up at the main gate waiting for his brother!" I told them that I was his brother. "How the heck did you get in here", they asked. I told them about the path and crossing the little draw. "How did you get past the sentry", they asked. I told them that I did not see a sentry. They were surprised. I was surprised also, since finding Bob's tent this soon, among the hundreds pitched on this hillside seemed something close to a miracle.

After getting directions to the main gate, I trotted up and met Bob! It was great to see him! I told Bob that I could spend the night and catch the landing craft back to Tinian the following afternoon. He moved an extra cot next to his in his tent.

Bob had guard duty that night, from midnight to 8: 00 AM and his buddy, Rogers, from Chicago, had agreed to stand it for him but needed their C.O.s approval. We went to talk to the C.O. and Bob introduced me. The C.O. refused to allow Rogers to stand Bob's watch and told us that he would not make any changes. I didn't like this guy! We went back to the tent and I suggested to Bob that I stand his watch with him so that we may visit and talk a little longer. It seemed like a good idea and Bob agreed. A film was being shown in camp that night and Rogers asked me to join them to see it. Bob said that he had to get some sleep before his watch so he didn't want to come. I joined Rogers and a couple of his friends to go watch the movie. Bob's C.O. was there and Rogers started to introduce me, when I told him that we had already met. The C.O. seemed annoyed that I was there and wanted to know what ship I was on. I told him that I was a member of the armed guard on the S.S. Fred Billings. He then asked, "How the hell did you get permission from you C.O. to come over here?" I grinned and said, "My C.O. is a prince of a guy, a real man, not a horses ass like some officers I've met!" I saw his neck turn red and for a moment, wondered if I had gone too far, but he just turned and walked away. I was a bit restless in these different surroundings and slept lightly. About 11:00 P.M. I heard carbine shots, which sounded very close! A few seconds later, I saw Bob roll over on his bunk, pick up his rifle, check the action and the cartridge clips, place the rifle down and turn back to sleep. A few minutes later, the tent flap was lifted and a marine whispered to Bob, "They got a problem on your watch, Rube!" "Did they get him?" Bob asked. "I don't think so!" was the answer. Bob then asked if I was awake. I said "No!" Bob then suggested that I not accompany him on his watch. I thought that was a good suggestion! I could envision a Merchant Sailor, in a navy uniform, not knowing passwords or procedures, either getting shot by some Marine or getting his throat cut by some Japanese on the North end of the island of Saipan! It was with a heavy heart that I watched Bob leave for his watch and slept no more that night! The next morning, I was standing in the chow line with Rogers, when I saw Bob, with his rifle slung over his shoulder, climbing up the hill. A big grin was on his face! I was sure glad to see him!

The visit meant much to me and Bob shared some snapshots which he had received from home. He said, "Just look at this picture of Tom, he has really grown and slimmed down! You know, I think he is going to kick the hell out of us when we get home, for being so mean to him at times!" I looked at the snapshots and agreed that Bob may be right!

I promised Bob that I would see him again, if our ship stopped at Saipan before going back to Pearl Harbor. I would arrange with the ship's cook to prepare the finest meal for Bob and his friends, if they could come down to the harbor.

I boarded the landing craft and started back to Tinian. As we neared Tinian Harbor, I searched anxiously for the masts of the Billings! My heart was beating wildly when we rounded the last point and my ship was not in the harbor! I quickly resigned myself to my problem. I gambled and lost, so I would simply seek out the officer in charge at Tinian, give him my story and accept the consequences!

The last turn of the landing craft into the harbor, allowed me to see the ship at the lone dock. It was the Billings and a Liberty ship never looked better to me! They had moved into the dock to unload our cargo of bombs. It had seemed, for a while, that the Air Force didn't want our one ton demolition bombs, since they were now using incendiary bombs. They finally agreed that our cargo be unloaded, but I doubt if those bombs were ever used. DeWayne and the crew told me that I had missed some excitement, in my absence! It seemed that, in unloading our bombs, a booby trap bomb was discovered in the number three hold, the same hold where the bomb rows were not wedged! They said our ship was moved out of the harbor until the device could be dismantled! I wasn't there, so I know only what others told me, someone in Calcutta had apparently tried to sabotage our ship and cargo.

When our cargo of bombs was unloaded, we sailed, stopping at Tanapaga Harbor at Saipan. I was disappointed that we would only be there several hours and I would not get to see Bob. I had "Beans" signal a message for him but I don't think he ever got it. When we rounded Saipan, heading north toward Pearl Harbor, I looked back toward Bob's camp at the hills on the North end of the island. I had a lonely feeling and missed all of my brothers and all at home!

A strange incident occurred about a week later at sea. I was in the crows nest on lookout near the end of my watch, at about 3:30 A.M., when suddenly I felt a movement, as though the ship hit a bump! I know there aren't any bumps at sea, but I reported it to the bridge. Doug Houston, the 2nd Mate, felt nothing! I had a strange feeling that something big had happened and when I finished my watch, I stopped at the bridge to discuss my feelings with the 2nd Mate. *I* told him how I felt and offered to bet him $20.00 that the war would be over by the time we reached Pearl Harbor! He gladly took the bet! I asked the gun crew and the others on watch, at the time, but none felt anything. I thought, perhaps, I felt some movement due to my position at the time, high on the foremast, in the crows nest. When we reached Pearl Harbor, I paid Doug the $20.00 bet, but less than 10 hours after we docked the news reported the surrender of Japan!

We realized that the celebration for V.J. Day in Honolulu may be hectic, so DeWayne Schwanke, Wayne Ulberg and I took advantage of the offer of a ranch cottage out of Honolulu. DeWayne's brother, Ray, in the Navy and stationed at Honolulu, had made friends with a navy supplier of dairy products. This supplier owned a dairy ranch and offered Ray and his friends, use of one of the cottages there. We occupied the cottage, celebrating with a few drinks, snacks and music while avoiding the wild crowds in town. The long World War 2 was over!

Our ship was scheduled to return to the South Pacific to pick up material and supplies, for return to the states, but an inspection of our propeller, slightly damaged in Calcutta, brought a cancellation of those plans. We then were ordered back to San Francisco.

Our crew celebrated, after docking in San Francisco. I consumed much too much whiskey and was mighty sick for several days. I recovered in time for the day scheduled for signing off and accepting the pay due me. I received $1700.00, the most money I ever had! The deck engineer, "Deck", with his dog, "Blackie", disappeared after we docked and didn't show up for the pay off. We learned that he owed more than $800.00 in gambling debts, to various members of the crew! Old "Deck" proved true to form and we had him pegged correctly!

***

DeWayne bought a 1938 Pontiac and two members of the engine crew, and I would accompany him as far as Omaha, on his trip home. I had previously met Milly, who later became DeWayne's wife, and Jeanette, Ray Schwanke's wife, and their sister, who were working at the ship yards and living in Richmond, California. We had dinner with them and started north. At Reno, Nevada, the clutch went out of his Pontiac, and we continued in 3rd gear, all the way to Elko, Nevada. We had the clutch repaired there, only to have it go out again less than 50 miles from Elko! We continued in 3rd gear to Salt Lake City, where DeWayne had to have the necessary repairs made. I said good-bye to DeWayne, since he was not going back to sea, but I would return to complete the necessary sea time to receive my Maritime Discharge.

The trip from Salt Lake City to St. Louis consisted of an ancient bus from Salt Lake City to Denver, a plane from Denver to Kansas City and a train from Kansas City to St. Louis. The train to St. Louis was crowded with standing room only. Fatigue got to me and I, along with several military personnel, lay in the aisle, next to the rest rooms. I was awakened, as people were stepping on my face, leaving the train in St. Louis. I was home!

My 30 day leave was spent sharing time at the farm and in Jennings. It was great being with Jane again and my brothers were all starting to arrive home. Mom's prayers had been answered, since all returned safely!

I returned to San Pedro and signed aboard a T-2 Tanker, the S.S. Salem Maritime. None of my old ship-mates were with me and I missed them, feeling somewhat alone with an entirely new crew. We loaded with 135,000 barrels of 100 Octane gas and delivered same to Pearl Harbor. From there we went to Panama, where I had the experience of steering the ship through the canal. We entered at Balboa, through the Miraflores Locks and Pedro Miquel Locks, then the Gaillard Cut into Gatun Lake, where we anchored overnight. The Gaillard Cut is 500 feet wide and 8 miles long, through solid rock, and the canal extends a little more than 50 miles. The next day we raised anchor and went through the Gatun Locks at Cristobal, on the Atlantic side.

We sailed North through the Gulf of Mexico, to Galveston, Texas. From Galveston, we sailed south through the Sargasso Sea to Aruba, in the Netherland West Indies. We took on a cargo of heating oil in Aruba and sailed north for delivery to New York. It was early December and the North Atlantic was bitter cold. Ice was thick on the mast shrouds, the bridge and most of the ship. I wore every bit of clothes I had with me and was still cold on watch! Lookout watches were stood on the "Flying Bridge", since the main deck, the cat walk and bow would often be covered with the heavy sea. We arrived in New York Harbor in a misty rain and anchored. The next morning, the rain ceased and, as the sky cleared, the beautiful Statue of Liberty became clearly visible through the parting mists!

DO-TELL

I wanted to be home for Christmas so I signed off the Salem Maritime and took a subway to Central Station, where I purchased a ticket to St. Louis. The ticket agent couldn't tell me what track the train would be leaving on and I had to wait in the terminal for the track to be announced. Central Station is a very large place and, when my train was announced, I had difficulty finding the track number. None of the attendants seemed to know where anything was and most seemed not to care! By the time I found my track, the train was already pulling out! This meant a six hour wait for the next train! I had a miserable headache and decided that I didn't like New York City or the people living there! I selected a bench in the terminal, sat down and fumed! I was on the bench a short while, when a well dressed , middle age man, wearing a camel hair overcoat, sat down next to me. Seeing my sea bag, he began to ask questions about how long I had been at sea, did I miss the girls and so on. I became suspicious! When he finally suggested that I come home with him to a nice warm bed, spend the night, and he would buy my dinner and breakfast and bring me back for my train the next day, I knew exactly what he was and could feel the blood rising in my neck! I turned to him and said, "This is the first time I've been in New York City, I don't like it here, I don't like the people, I missed my train and I have a sick headache! Just before you sat down, I mulled over all these things and said to myself, all I need now is for some fat, goddam queer to sit next to me and try to proposition me and I'll break his goddam arms!" The guy nearly fell on his face as he stumbled in his haste to depart from this mean, nasty sailor!

I was glad when I finally reached St. Louis. I was anxious to purchase a ring for Jane and ask her to marry me! She was everything I had hoped for and was excited about the future!

A few days before Christmas, Jane and I went to confession at Corpus Christi Church and, on the way back to her house, I parked the car on McLaren Avenue, presented Jane with the ring and asked her to marry me. We were both very happy but the date would have to be sometime in the future. I still had sea time due to earn sufficient points for my Maritime Discharge.

***

Aunt Annie told me that Mr. Naunheim wanted to see me about something and asked me to stop in at the bank. I couldn't imagine what he wanted, but stopped in the bank, the following day. He called me into his office and presented me with an envelope containing $500.00! I could hardly believe this, as I thanked him over and over! He said that the bank had a very profitable year and the Board of Directors agreed that Ed Jezik and I should also share in a bonus which was given to each member of the staff. I was very pleased and would always remember this generous gift!

I purchased a 1938 Chevrolet coupe for $636.00. It was a good looking auto but the engine was not so great. I kept this car a very short time and sold it, getting my $636.00 back. Price controls were still in effect and the figure for purchase and sale was the maximum under those controls.

***

Since Galveston, Texas was also a port from which I could sail, and much closer than California, I decided to go there and ship from the Gulf. I arrived in Galveston on a warm afternoon, in early January, and got a room at the old Southern Hotel, had supper and attended a movie, to pass the time. When the movie was over, I stepped out into a cold northern wind and was glad to get back to my hotel room. During the night *I* was awakened by some strange sounds, as if someone was trying to scratch at my transom and window. When I turned the light on, the noises would stop, but would start again as soon as the light was turned off. I finally left the light on and tried to sleep, while feeling insecure. At first daylight, I checked out and went to the shipping office, hoping for a ship which would sail soon. The dispatcher said that he had a Liberty ship needing an Able Bodied Seaman, and was ready to sail as soon as that position was filled. The crew had already signed articles and if I took the ship, I would have to go directly to the Company office and sign my articles. When I agreed to take the Liberty, the dispatcher told me that I would have to accept the duties of the crew representative since I would be the only one with an approved card from his office. This statement should have been sufficient warning to me, but I was anxious to ship, and blindly signed the articles and boarded the ship.

The ship was the S.S. Am Mer Mar, loaded with a cargo of wheat for delivery to Rotterdam, in the Netherlands. The ship was dirty, had not been hosed down since loading and wheat was growing in pockets in a number of areas! All hatches were battened and booms cradled, except the two booms on the number four hatch. These two booms remained rigged to unload the last bit of garbage to a scow which would be alongside soon. I was appalled when *I* met the crew, nearly all from the deep South and most sailing on temporary permits! I would be the only member of the deck crew with an Able Seaman Certificate, which meant that I would have to stand all wheel watches when the ship was under Pilot Control, entering and leaving port! Some members had been to sea only as messmen in the Stewarts Department, and the Bos'n sailed only once as an Ordinary Seaman! I knew that a serious shortage of experienced seamen existed, but I could hardly believe this! I went to the Chief Mate and expressed the concern that the inexperienced deck crew was a menace to the ship and to each other! He cut me short and didn't want to hear my comments! We then turned to on the number four hatch to discharge our garbage onto the scow which was now alongside. The crew was obviously not familiar with the operation of the winches, and most of the garbage was dumped on the deck! When we finally cleaned everything up and the scow cast off the mate ordered us to lower and cradle the remaining two number 4 booms. The bos'n started ordering the crew to positions and it was evident that he didn't know what he was doing! The chief mate was standing on the boat deck and I glanced up at him, hoping that he would intercede. He didn't! The attempt to lower the first boom ended in near disaster as control was lost and the boom crashed onto the railing of the boat deck, not 10 feet from where the First Mate stood! That did it! I immediately went up to the mate and told him to either get some experienced men in the crew or let me off the ship! He refused to do either, although he was visibly shaken! Seamen's law states that a seaman can be released from his contract (the articles of agreement) if the Captain agrees to the release. It is called the "Mutual Consent Agreement". I went to see the Captain, expressed my fears and concerns, and asked to be signed off under the agreement. He became rather indignant and refused! He was from Rotterdam and spoke with a heavy Dutch accent. When I tried further comments on the inexperience of his deck crew, his face turned red and he slammed his fist on the table saying, "Tomorrow morning at 0600 the "Am Mer Mar" is sailing out of this harbor on our voyage to Rotterdam!" I know I was cocky and combative, but I was also very angry, as I snapped, "Tomorrow morning at

0600, when the S.S. Am Mer Mar sails out of this harbor I'll be standing on the dock, with my sea bags and I'll be waving goodbye to you!" He ordered me out of his office and I went to my focile and started to pack my sea bag, preparing to leave. I was nearly finished when the Chief Mate came to my door, told me to call a cab and the Captain would accompany me to the company office to sign me off under the "Mutual Consent Agreement". It was a quiet ride to the company office with the Captain but I got my release!

I had enough of the Southern ports and went back to St. Louis for a few days before going to San Pedro on the West coast. I was not too surprised, some months later, when Jane gave me a newspaper clipping about the sinking of the S.S. Am Mer Mar! The ship hit some rocks near Norway, broke up and sunk, with all of the crew being rescued. I don't think the sinking occurred on the voyage I was to make, but was probably on a subsequent trip. At any rate, I was glad that I was not a part of that strange crew!

***

When I arrived in San Pedro, the dispatcher told me that the U.S. Government had given four "Baby Liberty Ships" to the Chinese Nationalists and were offering a special deal to entice crews to deliver same to China. They would pay $200.00 per month, tax free, and provide first class transportation back to the states. The ships had been at anchor for many months and were now being readied for sea. The "Baby Liberty" ships looked like a regular Liberty without the last two hatches. The ship had three holds forward and ended with the superstructure aft. They were designed for inter-island use during the war but had proven to be a sub-standard vessel. They were very slow, about 5 or 6 knots, and would sometimes break up in a heavy sea. I had met another Able Seaman in San Pedro and we were sharing a room near the shipping office. Both of us had run out of funds and were sneaking food from various ships in the harbor. We both agreed to work aboard the Baby Liberty. When we boarded the vessel, it appeared rather spooky, the last crew left the ship in some haste, with clothing scattered in the fociles and unwashed dishes in the mess hall and galley. We started the clean up and repair. The ship was then renamed the S.S. Hai Ling and moved to a dry dock for sand blasting and modifications. At the dry dock, workers began welding a steam pipe all around the gunwale of the ship, with jets placed about 2 feet apart. Controls for the steam pipe were run to the bridge. I asked a workman about the pipes and their purpose. He told me that they had installed this same apparatus on one Baby Liberty before, and it was for protection against pirates on the river in China! He said that the vessels, moving cargo up the river, had to anchor at night during low tide and Chinese river pirates would board, capture the ship and crew and steal the cargo! He said that large flood lights were to be installed on the mainmast, so that a lookout, from the bridge, could activate the scalding steam jets as the pirates attempted to board! Sounded wild to me but I believe he was telling the truth since I could see no other purpose for the installation!

After several weeks, the proposed "Articles of Agreement" were posted on the board in the mess hall. I read the entire agreement. We estimated that the trip over to China would take no more than 60 days, and expected our agreement to run for 90 days. Instead it called for 36 months, during which time we would be under option to the Chinese Government for the purposes of training the crew in the operation and maintenance of the vessel. When my friend and I explained the contents of the "Agreement" to the temporary crew, very few wanted to sign. *I* sure didn't want to contract for 36 months on some Chinese river watching for river pirates! Several seamen and I refused to sign and went back to the dispatcher. I Learned later that two of the four Baby Liberty ships broke up, one between San Pedro and San Francisco and the other between San Francisco and Pearl Harbor. I don't know if the S.S. Hai Ling was one of them

***

I visited Aunt May, in El Monte, for two days, and then accepted an assignment on a new T-2 Tanker, the S.S. Whittier Hills. It had completed its shakedown cruise and was declared ready for cargo and sea duty. She proved to have a few serious "bugs" remaining.

The crew of the S.S. WHITTIER HILLS was a good one and I became good friends with several in all departments. I was on board for several days when a bos'n was assigned to the ship, a 63 year old Swede, named Fred Berglund, who had been sailing since he was 12 years old. Fred was a very capable seaman when he was sober and a real menace when not. An Australian, Jack Potts, shared Fred's quarters, sailing as Deck Maintenance. My watch partners were Bill Taylor and Clyde Kliss, both great guys from California. T-2 tankers carried four men for each watch, adding a Quartermaster, who stood 3 1/2 hours of each watch on the wheel. Once again, I was appointed the delegate to represent the crew.

I met the Chief Engineer a few days before we sailed, John Buckley, who had studied in the Jesuit Seminary and left the order shortly before his scheduled ordination. He was a friendly, talkative officer and we became good friends. The Captain was a very quiet, moody man and the Chief Mate, a Norwegian named John Jensen, was not the best liked officer.

All in all, the crew was experienced and I looked forward to our sailing date.

We took on 135,000 barrels of gasoline and kerosene and sailed from San Pedro. The bos'n was drunk and stayed in his quarters for four or five days. Jack Potts took over running the deck crew, in his absence. I took Fred some food and tried to get him to eat, while I lectured him on his drinking. When he finally sobered up, he was a reasonable, competent sailor and would tell tales of his 51 years at sea, a number of his early years being on sailing vessels. He promised that he would do no more drinking on our voyage.

While I was relieving on wheel watch, several nights at sea, the Chief Mate asked me if I had met the Chief Engineer, John Buckley. I told him that I had. He then proceeded to tell me he had first met him when he came aboard, and found that there was something about him that he didn't like, but couldn't put his finger on it until that very day. He went on to tell me, "Ruby, that son of a bitch is a Catholic! Now let me tell you, if there is one thing in this world you can't trust, it is a rotten Catholic! They are the most treacherous no-good bastards in the world!" When he finally paused long enough for me to speak, I said, "Mate, I want you to know that I am a Catholic!" The mate had been pacing back and forth in the wheel house, as he spoke, and was near a port hole when I made my statement. He froze, stood perfectly still for some time and then said, "Son of a bitch Ruby, you don't look like a Catholic!" The remaining time I spent on wheel watch that night was very quiet. Strangely, during the rest of our voyage, the Chief Mate was quite friendly to me and never once did he again mention Catholics.

Several days later, a serious problem became evident as the engines failed! T-2 tankers were equipped with electrical turbine generators, of which I knew nothing. The Chief Engineer, Buckley, was an expert, however, and the breakdown was usually repaired within a few hours. When the engines went out, a long whine preceded dead silence. The whine became a familiar sound, as we broke down 17 times between San Pedro and Sydney, Australia.

Fred Berglund fished for shark during the depression years of the 1930's and watched the waters for shark each time the ship broke down. He had us contain the garbage on the fan tail of the ship, dumping it when the engine failed. It seemed unlikely that we would see shark in this vast area but, when the engines failed several miles north of the Equator, we dumped the garbage and rubbish and were surprised to see huge shark swarming toward our ship! They would even grab orange crates, dive deep with the crates in their mouth, bite them into shreds and the splintered crates would float to the surface! The water was crystal clear and visibility was at least 100 feet deep! Someone in the engine crew had made a large hook, to which we fastened line, baited it with 1/2 of a frozen turkey and dropped it over the stern. Several shark attacked at once, with the largest grabbing the bait. When we hauled the shark up, we couldn't get it over the rail, so one of the seamen grabbed a fire axe and began striking it in the head , using the pointed end. The shark struggled and tore loose, with blood streaming everywhere. I watched the trail of blood as it dove deep, with several shark right behind it. We baited the hook again and tossed it over. I could hardly believe it, as I saw the same wounded shark turn and speed to the new bait, taking it savagely! This time we had this 8 foot 2 inch shark! We caught a total of seven and the bos'n asked me to help him extract the livers from the female sharks. He said we would sell them when we returned to the states and split the money.

We carefully stored the livers in the freezer and cut a number of shark steaks for future meals. The fan tail of the ship was covered with blood and I was glad when the engines were started so we could wash down the deck and get under way! With a number of the crew slipping and sliding on the fan tail, in their excitement, I feared someone would lose their footing, slip over the rail and be a shark dinner!

***

Before our ship left San Pedro, a salesman from the Coca Cola Bottling Company came aboard to persuade someone to purchase Coca Cola to take along on our voyage and resell same at a profit. He offered the Coke at 90 cents per case of 24 bottles, plus a deposit of 88 cents a case for the bottles. Most thought it was a good idea but few had any money. Since I had my pay from the S.S.HAI LING, I agreed to buy 70 cases, sell them to members of the crew for $1.20 a case (5 cents a bottle), and when I returned the bottles for recovery of my deposit, I would make 30 cents per case for a total of $21.00. This profit, together with the money the Bos'n and I were to make on the shark livers would just be like found money! It didn't work out that way! Since almost all of my coca cola sales were on credit, I failed to collect from everyone and found it impossible to return the empty bottles when we finally returned home. My business enterprise resulted in a loss. Thus began my long personal business career of "buying high and selling low!" In addition, the shark livers were still on board when I paid off the S.S. Whittier Hills.

***

We continued the voyage, with periodic breakdowns. When we were less than 300 miles from Sydney, we encountered a storm with heavy seas. Someone had just stated that this would be a bad time to break down, when that familiar whine was heard. We were adrift without power! As we began a Northerly drift, concern increased due to the close proximity of the reefs off the coast of Australia! We radioed for help and a sea going tug was dispatched from Sydney. We, in the deck crew, began the arduous task of preparing the ship for towing, while the engine crew worked around the clock, attempting repairs. We lowered a seaman over the starboard bow to secure a cable to the flukes of the starboard anchor. When this was done, we cabled the anchor to the starboard bits to prevent it from dropping, as we pulled up the anchor chain with blocks and tackle. Each link of the chain weighed 55 pounds and the entire chain was removed from the chain locker, unshackled from the bottom of the ship, and flaked along the deck. The unshackled end was then pulled up the port side and placed at the chalk on the port bow. When the tug arrived, they would take that end and tow us with our own anchor chain! When all was completed, we received a radio message that the tug developed engine trouble and was returning to Sydney! We continued the drift North at four knots. We later received a message that the tug was repaired and had left Sydney. The next report came from the tug, requesting assistance, they were struggling in heavy seas and one of their officers had received a concussion from being thrown about. They were trying to get back to Sydney or into Brisbane! We then knew that we were on our own!

Chief Engineer, Buckley, called ship's emergency and all available deck crew were requested to come below to assist. Eight of us from the deck crew went below to find parts of equipment all over the engine room floor! I wondered how the Chief Engineer would ever get it all back together. The

Chief said that the condenser tubes were leaking salt water into the boiler system and the tubes had to be cleaned. The inspection plates were removed from the condenser tubes, providing an opening just large enough for a man to squeeze through. A Hawaiian, Dave Kapuko, and I stripped to our shorts, squeezed through and began the task of cleaning the salt out of thousands of little evaporator holes. The feeling of claustrophobia was sneaking up on me, as I commented to Dave that I hoped that someone had closed the sea valve which allowed sea water into the tubes! He was laughing at my comment when the ship rolled hard to port and spilled many gallons of water from the intake lines to the tube! We both made a jump for the hole, to exit the tube, but Dave beat me there! He left a lot of skin on the inspection entrance as he squeezed out! I was right behind him! We checked the valves, finding that they were closed and the water we got was just lying in the feeder lines. We entered the tubes again and finally, after many hours, completed the task. The Chief said that there was nothing further for the deck crew to do so we could return to the deck. We barely had strength enough to climb the ladder back to the deck! We had been working straight through, without sleep, for over 36 hours, but many in the engine crew had been working even longer!

Back on deck, the Chief Mate ordered me on the flying bridge to call out the distance from the Middleton Reef, a part of the Great Barrier Reef. I could see the waves breaking over the reef! The Captain wanted to delay dropping the anchor, since we now had but one ready and it was questionable if one would hold in this heavy sea. Once dropped, if power was not restored, it could not be retrieved. The decision was made to wait and hope for a change in the wind or engine repairs completed. I called out less than 10 miles with continued drifting toward the reef! Everyone was becoming anxious! When we were less than a mile from the reef, the wind suddenly shifted, and we started to drift northeast, away from the reef! Several hours later, the engines were started and we turned back toward Sydney, cruising at only 6 knots. We had drifted nearly 400 miles since the breakdown.

We entered the harbor at Sydney on Good Friday and were greeted by a flotilla of nearly every type of boat, crowded with waving and cheering Australians! We learned that we had been at the top of all news reports, for a number of days, and many were applauding our safe arrival! I had never been so tired in my life!

***

All businesses were closed on Easter weekend and I stood security watch, on board, until Easter Sunday morning, when I went ashore to attend mass at St. Mary's Cathedral. We discharged part of our cargo and remained in port while the necessary repairs were made to the condenser and evaporator.

When shore liberty expired and we readied for sea, Bill Taylor, my watch partner, was missing. He had not returned from a date the previous night! I went to the captain and asked him to delay departure and he agreed to delay for 10 minutes. Bill had not returned at the end of the 10 minutes and we were ordered to take in the gangway and prepare for sea! I went to the captain again and asked for time, but he refused. I went back to our deck crew and told them to delay any way they could! This angered both the mate and the Captain! I then reminded the Captain, under Seamen's law, a missing seaman's gear must be placed on the dock, before we could sail. He ordered me to assemble his gear and place it on the dock! I delayed and the Chief Mate stormed into our focile demanding to know what was keeping me. I had placed a padlock on Bill's locker and told the mate that I had no key. "Break the lock and get his gear on the dock!" he snapped. When he left I produced a key and stuffed Bill's gear into his sea bag. My heart was heavy, since Bill and I had become good friends. I took the bag on deck and assisted in taking in the gangway. Suddenly, a taxi careened onto the dock, Bill jumped out and raced to the ship! We scolded him and told him that we were about to be logged for not obeying orders. I was sure glad that he was back on board!

We sailed from Sydney to Brisbane to discharge the remaining portion of our cargo and received orders to go to Abadan, Iran and then Bahrein, in the Persian Gulf, to take on a cargo of crude. After leaving Brisbane, we set a course for the Persian Gulf, which meant a voyage back through the Coral Sea, the Arafura Sea and Timor Sea, North of Australia, past Java and Sumatra, across the Indian Ocean, then North along the West coast of India to the Persian Gulf! A long trip!

After passing through the Coral Sea and rounding the Northern tip of Australia, we entered the Arafura Sea. We then received a radio message changing our orders since there seemed to be some threatening problems with the Soviet Union in the area of the Persian Gulf. We were directed to reverse our course and return to Cairns, Australia, for orders. At Cairns, we were ordered to sail to Suva in the Figi Islands.

The Figi Islands were fascinating to me and I enjoyed our stop there. The natives, many of whom had been head hunters only 50 years before, were very friendly, happy people. The men were tall, well built and handsome, with large, bushy heads of hair. We called them "Fuzzy Wuzzies". The women were homely, with drooping earlobes, lips and other things. On my first day ashore with Jack Potts, we were walking down the street in Suva, and saw two homely women walking along, carrying baskets on their heads. They were bare from the waist up; their breasts drooped to near their waist and appeared "dusty." They had large rings in their ears and one had a large ring in one nostril! Jack grabbed my arm exclaiming, "Rube, that one on the right is not too bad!" I thought he was a little nuts and urged him to keep moving!

Bos'n Fred kept his promise of no drinking while we were in Australia, but the plentiful supply of good scotch whiskey at bargain prices, in Suva, proved too much for him and others in our crew! When sailing time was drawing near, we were alarmed to find that Bos'n Fred and a member of the engine crew were missing! Bill Taylor and I set out to look for Fred and found him, stone drunk, lying between some crates at the rear of a warehouse. We carried him back to the ship, as I wondered just how much longer the Captain would put up with Fred's drinking. The engine crew member was never found and we sailed without him!

Bos'n Fred had purchased enough scotch whiskey to remain well stoned throughout our entire trip to Panama and I sensed that he would not be with us very much longer. Upon reaching Balboa, we learned that another T-2 tanker was to come alongside to exchange some supplies, and I was asked to build a small catwalk, with rails, which could be placed between the two ships. I completed the project and was rather pleased with my very limited building skills. The tanker came alongside, when we were anchored outside of Balboa and, after tying up, we brought out the catwalk to place same between the two vessels. Bos'n Fred then appeared on deck, half drunk and started giving senseless orders! The skipper and mate, from the other ship, were standing on their deck watching and I saw the expression on our Captain's face. He ordered

Fred back to his quarters but Fred refused to go! With that, several of our deck crew grabbed Fred and took him back to his quarters! I knew then that Fred would be fired in Panama! When we reached the dock near the entrance to the Canal, we had an overnight wait and spent the evening in Panama City. The next morning Fred was fired, his gear placed on the dock, and we started our trip through the locks and canal. He was a pathetic sight! As we pulled away, I looked back and saw him standing next to his belongings, watching us leave. I could not help feeling sorry for this old drunken sailor! I also thought of all those shark livers in the freezer and knew that is where they would stay!

Jack Potts was then promoted to Bos'n and I was promoted to Deck Maintenance to replace Jack. .Jack and I would share quarters and would both serve as replacements for any deck member who was sick or injured and could not stand watch. We also hired two men from South America, one to fill the vacancy when I was promoted and one to replace our engine crew member lost in Suva. Neither spoke English very well, were funny, and we enjoyed having them for the rest of our voyage.

We sailed to Aruba, in the Netherland West Indies and took on a cargo of gasoline. Our course through the Caribbean and Sargasso Sea was always fascinating as I marveled at the floating grass islands and watched the beautiful phosphorus roll deep in the waters, from our wake at night. One night I had to stand a crow's nest watch, for a sick seaman, and was startled to see strange, moving lights in the sky, around the ship, darting back and forth and up and down! I couldn't imagine what this was but promptly reported it to the bridge. The Captain called me back in a few minutes, telling me that these were SEA BIRDS which had picked up so much phosphorus in their feathers, that they produced this glowing light as they turned in flight! Amazing!

***

From Aruba, we sailed across the Atlantic toward the Mediterranean, our destination being Savona, in Northern Italy. About a day out of Gibralter, the lookout called out an object floating near dead ahead. The ship's helm was put to starboard and we passed a floating mine! It apparently had broken from it anchorage somewhere and was now adrift at sea. It looked rather menacing, with all of its spikes encrusted with barnacles! Our officers radioed its position and we continued our course. The war was over and all guns had been removed from our ship, so there was nothing we could do with that floating menace.

We reached Savona and anchored in the harbor, a mile from shore. The wind was brisk and there appeared to be a very strong current, so it was necessary that we drop both anchors. There were no actual docks at Savona, so our gasoline would be discharged through a floating pipe extended several hundred yards into the harbor. Another ship was discharging when we arrived, so we would have to await our turn.

The crew was anxious to go ashore, so I volunteered to stand "security watch" and remained aboard. I didn't like to go ashore the first night in any port, since many would drink too much, get into fights and wind up in trouble. Some Italians, in row boats, came alongside and offered to take anyone ashore who wanted to go. They rowed the mile out and back for a very modest fee, often for just several packs of American cigarettes.

The ship had but a skeleton crew left on board, with me being the only member of the deck crew remaining. About 10:30, I was reading in my quarters, when someone knocked on the door. I opened the door and was surprised to see three Italian men, one of whom spoke English, introduced himself as Ferrari Giuseppi, and asked to come in. We sat down as he told me that he wanted to buy 1000 gallons of gasoline at $1.00 per gallon, American money, or if I preferred he would pay in Italian Lira. With that, he opened a small suitcase and showed me stacks of American and Italian currency. All three were armed and I didn't want to irritate or offend them. I asked them how they intended to get 1000 gallons of gasoline off our ship. They said their boat, equipped with a large tank, was tied along the port side of our ship, just forward of the superstructure. They wanted me to drop a heaving line to them, pull up their hoses, and fill their tank from our port tanks by gravity flow. I wasn't about to challenge them, so I said, "You don't need me, just take your hoses and get the gasoline yourself!" Ferrari looked at me and said, "No, my friend, I want to buy it, I do not steal!" I looked him straight in the eye as I said, "This gasoline does not belong to me and I have no authority to sell any of it. You see, I DON'T STEAL EITHER!" He looked at me for a while, then smiled and shook my hand. We walked back to the port side where they boarded their boat and left. I met this man several times while we were in port and he told me that he operated a black market ring and would be pleased to buy large quantities of American cigarettes, soap or nylon stockings, if we were to return. I became to like this guy and realized what a profit one could make legitimately if he wanted to continue sailing during this post war period. I was not interested since I was anxious to complete my sea time and return home.

Most of the crew went to Milano, a town South of Savona, for shore liberty. There, was a popular bar there, operated by a widow and her two daughters, both of whom were quite aggressive and often joined us at our table. Both smelled strongly of garlic! One Saturday, several of us were seated at a table having some cognac, when the monastery bells began ringing. One of the girls grabbed me by the hand and said that we should run to watch the feast day procession. We ran a few blocks, to an intersection, and watched as a group of robed monks approached, carrying the Blessed Sacrament beneath a white canopy. All knelt as the procession passed and I was impressed with their devotion. On the way back to the tavern, the girl said, "I like you, I talked with Momma and she said I could sleep with you tonight, provided that I get to mass on time tomorrow morning!" I could hardly believe what she was saying and answered, "You are a nice girl, but I don't want to sleep with you, I have a very special girl at home, who is waiting for me!" She seemed disappointed but accepted my answer. We continued back to the tavern as I pondered the strange customs and standards of so many of our foreign friends.

Many of our crew had no inhibitions about sleeping with girls, and our ship seemed over run with Italian girls at times. I didn't like the idea of them being on board and had never encountered this in any port before. I was shocked, as I went to take a shower one day, and nearly bumped into a nude girl stepping out of one of our showers! She just smiled and continued back to her friend! I was pleased when we had orders to take in the anchors and move to Milano, to discharge the remaining portion of our gasoline. When we brought up the anchors, however, the two anchors were locked together! The ship had swung far in the current and wind, and somehow the anchors crossed, with the fluke of one locked into the other. We tried for several hours to separate the anchors, which could be hoisted only to the surface of the water. We finally slipped a cable around one anchor, and by raising and dropping the other, separated the two. It was a freak happening!

The night before we sailed from Milano, Chief Engineer, John Buckley, got into a fight with one of his Engineers and the Chief's jaw was broken. He was treated in Milano, came back on board and we sailed. After only a short time at sea, Buckley's jaw became infected and he was very ill. We stopped at Barcelona, Spain, and the Captain wanted to put Chief Buckley ashore there for hospital treatment, but he refused, saying he would be OK until we reached the states. Before reaching Gibralter, however, his infection became much worse and he was running a high fever. We radioed for a medical vessel to meet us at Gibralter, and the Captain ordered maximum speed from the engines. I went to Buckley's quarters to see him. I hardly recognized him, his head appeared twice its normal size and his lips were so swollen that he could barely talk. He asked for a cigarette so I lighted one for him and placed it in his lips. I soon had to remove it, since the burning end would drop toward the side and begin to burn his flesh, but he didn't seem to feel it! We made contact with the medical ship and met them off Gibralter. John Buckley was unconscious as we lowered him, in a stretcher basket, over the side and onto the waiting ship. Several months later, when I was home, I wrote to him at his address in California but received no answer so I don't know what ever happened to him!

As the weather cooled, in the Atlantic, Jack Potts and I moved our quarters to the radio operator's quarters on the boat deck, since we no longer had a radio operator and these quarters were not occupied. This gave us more comfortable quarters on one deck above the main deck. We started to gas free the tanks, using steam "Butterworth" equipment and wind sails. The sails would capture the air, forcing it down through a canvas funnel into the tanks to push the lighter gas fumes out. After nearly a week, the tanks were not gas free, so we took turns going down into the tanks and scraping rust pockets with a wooden scraper. Safety lines were attached to each man since it was hazardous duty and one could be easily overcome. In order to determine the effect of the fumes, we would regularly look up, from the bottom of the tank, into the tank opening and when the opening would appear to waiver or become hazy, it was time to get out! We finally succeeded in getting all tanks gas free!

***

There is a saying that "You never know a man until you go to sea with him!" How true! One's irritating habits which would be ignored on shore can become overpowering after a long sea voyage! An able seaman on the Whittier Hills, named Hank, on the 8 to 12 watch, had more than a few irritating habits. He smoked constantly while awake, even as he ate his food. He chewed with his mouth open and drooled! For some reason, he took a liking to me and always tried to have his mess hall at the same time with me. When I delayed coming to chow, he would come looking for me. His morning watch and my day watch began at the same time, making it impossible for me to avoid him at breakfast. The menu for each day was written on a blackboard in the mess room and our orders were taken by a mess man from the Stewards Department. Each morning Hank would order scrambled eggs. This was no problem until he smeared mustard all over the eggs! It looked awful! He would always sit next to me or opposite me while smoking,, chewing,, drooling and smearing mustard on his eggs! After a while I couldn't stand him and just wanted to punch his lights out! I thought I had reached a breaking point one morning and prayed that he would be late for chow. It never happened! I knew when he said, "Pass the mustard", I was going to clobber him! He sat opposite me that morning and ordered his usual, scrambled eggs. I felt my muscles tense! The he yelled, "PASS THE MUSTARD!" In a flash, a crew member from the engine crew, seated next to me, lunged across the table, grabbed Hank by the shirt, jerked him upright and shouted, "You son of a bitch, if you smear mustard on your eggs, I'm going to kill you!" The engine crew man then jumped up and left the mess hall. Hank turned white, just looked at me with such a pathetic expression and said, "Gee Rube, what did I do to him?" I now felt ashamed and sorry for Hank as I answered, "Hank, I guess he just couldn't stand to see you put mustard on your scrambled eggs. It does look awful and must bother some people!" He never knew my feelings and never used mustard again!

***

When we reached Cristobal, at the Atlantic side of the Panama Canal, we awaited our turn to enter the locks. When we received approval to enter, we started slowly toward the locks, about 1/2 mile distant. Jack and I took our positions on the bow to stand by the anchors. We removed the "devil claws" on both anchors so they would be ready to drop in an emergency. We had done this so many times that it became routine, but we never had to drop an anchor in an emergency. As we stood by, Jack decided to go back to the mess hall for a cup of coffee and I would stand the anchor watch alone, until he returned. He had been gone but a short time when that old familiar whine of the failed engine reached my ears! The pilot on the bridge yelled, "Drop the starboard hook!" I quickly released the anchor brake, and the anchor began its noisy clatter to the ocean floor! Over the clatter, I heard the pilot yell, "Drop the port hook!" I repeated the process and both hooks were down! Jack ran back to the bow, yelling, "What the devil happened?" I told him and we decided that we would both remain at our stations for any future approaches! The Panama Security Patrol speeded out and came aboard our vessel. They were upset and, after much discussion, refused to allow us through the canal until proof of repairs would be accepted. The engines were started again, after several hours, but they refused acceptance, fearing loss of control of the ship with damage to the locks or the canal. We then received orders to go to Galveston, Texas.

We steered North, through the Gulf and entered Galveston Harbor where we anchored to await directions. The next day, the crew was allowed shore leave but I volunteered to stand security watch again, due to my continued concern for that first night ashore! The Chief Mate and I were the only members of the deck crew on board, when we received a radio message that another T-2 tanker would be coming alongside to take off our bunker fuel supply, since our vessel was then scheduled for a lengthy stay in port for repairs. The Chief and I talked and agreed that it was impossible to tie up, fore and aft, with the approaching tanker, with only the two of us! We then found two mess men who agreed to assist us, one on the bow with me and one at the stern with the Chief Mate. I briefed my mess-man as the tanker came alongside. We worked frantically, but all went well and we were finally secured. I looked up as I heard the Chief Mate on the other tanker call my name. It was the Chief Mate from the S.S. SALEM MARITIME, and he yelled, "Ruby, I thought that were you, I told my men that there were few men who worked that hard and did their job so well, you can sail with me anytime!" I consider his comments to be one of the finest compliments I ever received! Our "anti-Catholic" Chief Mate came up to the bow and we shook hands, feeling pretty good about getting the job done! The two mess-men had proven to be willing and hard working additions to our stations.

We docked and, in a few days, were called together for our final pay off for the voyage. We received an extra $10.00 per month when sailing tankers, due to the hazards related to the cargo. I accepted my pay, took a bus to Houston and caught a plane to St. Louis. The necessary sea time had now been served and I was eligible for my Maritime Discharge. Jane met me at the airport in St. Louis. It was good to be home!

***

I stopped at the bank to deposit my last pay and to draw some money for a long awaited vacation. When Mr. Naunheim saw me, he said, "Welcome home, my boy, we're so glad you're out, we really need some help! Just step into your old teller's window and go to work!" I told him that I had just arrived that day and planned to take a vacation. He said that I could vacation some other time, but right now they needed me. I went to my old teller's window and went to work!

About a week later, I had a telephone call from Clyde Kliss, in California. Clyde was a good friend on my watch on the S.S. WHITTIER HILLS. He told me that he had my shipping pass and was waiting for me to come out to California to ship with him. My heart was heavy as I told him "No". I loved the sea but I was more in love with a pretty girl, with a sweet smile and disposition and we hoped to marry soon! Clyde tried to persuade me but finally realized that he would not be successful!

Mr. Naunheim had told me that my salary would be decided by the Board of Directors, who then met each Monday. I was making $135.00 per month when I left for the Merchant

Marine, so I hoped for a good increase to help with our marriage plans. Jane was working for the Civil Service and was making $200.00 per month. Weeks passed, and then months, with no further 'mention of my salary! Finally, when I had exhausted most of my savings, I asked Mr. Naunheim when the Board would decide my salary. He promised that it would be done at the next Monday Board meeting. Following that meeting, he told me that I would be paid $165.00 per month, $40.00 more than I was making more than 2 years before. I then received my back pay for the months since I returned. I had hoped for a larger raise and was disappointed, but said nothing. I liked Mr. Naunheim and had confidence in my future.

Jane and I set a date of February 8, 1947, for our wedding. This time would work well for her parents, who would not be busy with planting and gardening at that time. I had purchased a 1942 Pontiac sedan for $1300.00, after receiving my back pay from the bank, but sold it when we set our wedding date. We wanted to find a house to buy and needed the money for a down payment and furniture. We agreed that I could walk to work and we could take the bus where we needed or wanted to go.

The months before our wedding were busy ones. We made plans and visited my family in Chesterfield, in their new home. Pop retained 2 acres, at the bottom of our hill, and sold the rest of the old hill farm to Ray and Nonnie Alsbury, from St. Louis. All my brothers built the new house, which had electricity and a pump for water from the cistern. It also had a real bath! Mom waited a long time, but she finally had life just a little easier.

In November, Mary and Harry Davis were married. Father Godfrey performed the ceremony with Tudor as Maid of Honor and I as Best Man. We were all happy with our new

Brother in Law and felt that both had made a good choice! Harry liked to fish and that also pleased me!

In January, the Board of Directors approved a raise of $60.00 per month for me, bringing my monthly salary to $225.00. This really helped and we were excited about our plans for a home and future!

The long awaited day for our wedding finally arrived. The Saturday of February 8, 1947 dawned clear and cold with temperatures at 8 degrees above zero. The heating system at Corpus Christi failed during the previous night and we all shivered from the cold, as we participated at mass and said our vows.

When Father Blankenmeier gave the last blessing, we turned from the altar and took our first step in our long journey as husband and wife, parents and grandparents, but that is ANOTHER STORY!

***

TO JANE
THE ROAD I CHOSE

Two roads diverged on the path of life
The path laid out for me,
One road would lead me to your arms,
The other to the sea
###
The ocean spray does penetrate
Grinds deep into ones soul
I longed to feel the ocean breeze
And the deck beneath me roll.

The care-free life of the open sea

On the road across the blue
Beckoned long and called to me
But I chose the road to you!

In my dreams I saw you waiting
With dampened eyes and anxious heart
I prayed dear God to speed me faster
Home to you, to never part.

Long before our wedding vows
Long before God made us one
I promised that I'd keep you happy
Until our task on earth was done.

Since the day we left the altar
Arm in arm as man and wife
My love for you increases daily
And shall grow for all my life.

When darkened clouds pass o'er our heavens
To swallow up the blue
Our love and trust in God will conquer
And light again will filter through

As summer fades into the Autumn
And seasons of our life do pass
The bridge that we have built together
Will join our love until the last

When our lips are sealed forever
And our eyes no longer see
I pray our God to permit us
To join Him in eternity.

Two roads diverged on the path of life
A choice we all must make
If I could live my life anew
The same road, I would take!

I sharpened my hoe good and sharp, this morning, planning to chop some Canadian thistles from the ridge field and the meadow below the dam. The fields seem larger lately and the hills much steeper. I tired on my way back and sat beneath the oak trees, by the lake to rest a bit. As I closed my eyes, I thought of long ago, on the old hill farm. I could see Pop and the "boys" grubbing stumps from the field for our new strawberry patch, hear Pop yell, "Eeeyahh!" at the team, hear their traces rattle as they squatted and strained for the pull. I could see pretty Mary, sitting on the old wood cistern box, waiting for everyone to come to supper, see the long and short benches around the table and everyone ready to eat. I knew that I was just dreaming and would have to wait for the time when Pop, Mom, and the entire family would all be together again, including Little Jess, the brother whom I'd never met!

***

As I started again for the house, I mentally reviewed my day dreaming memories, debating whether or not to share them with Jane. The wind picked up and from somewhere, I seemed to hear a vaguely familiar voice, a voice from long ago, the voice of a sweet little old black lady, and she was saying something! It sounded like, "DO TELL! DO TELL!"

We can never go back and re-capture the past, but as long as blood pumps through our veins, we have the opportunity to finally succeed in some matters, which were undertaken but not completed, many years ago!

Some hot, still summer night I, therefore, shall take Jane to a large cornfield. We'll hold hands as we walk to the center of the field and stand there quietly. I'll be smiling as Jane exclaims, "JUST LISTEN TO THAT CORN GROWING!"

THE END.

Made in the USA
San Bernardino, CA
05 April 2014